MEDIA MANUALS

The Animation Stand

MEDIA MANUALS

The Animation Stand

ROSTRUM CAMERA OPERATION

Zoran
Perisic

Focal Press · London

Focal/Hastings House · New York

ISBN (excl. USA) 0 240 50863 7
ISBN (USA only) 0 8038 03869

First edition 1976
Second impression 1980

Printed and bound in Great Britain by A. Wheaton & Co. Ltd, Exeter

Contents

Introduction

In recent years the animation stand has come to be used more and more in film and T.V. production. There cannot be a viewer who has not seen something shot on one unless they never see titles sequences, optical effects, commercials, or just plain cartoon animation. The chances are that anything which looks 'tricky' or makes a viewer wonder "how did they do that?" — is likely to have gone through at least one stage which involved the use of an animation stand, if indeed, it has not been shot entirely on it.

In Britain, the camera used is called a *rostrum camera.* In simplest terms it can be any motion picture camera equipped for stop-motion photography and mounted on a stand (usually vertical). The camera and the stand is known in the U.S.A. as the *animation stand.* Zooming (or more precisely 'tracking') is achieved by moving the camera towards the subject being photographed; but for "panning" it is the subject which is moved in a plane 90° to the axis along which the camera travels.

This book ranges from the simplest ways in which existing equipment can be adapted to shoot animation or titles, to the much more sophisticated cameras and stands presently in use. The intention is to stimulate the reader to experiment and work out his own solutions to the problems that he may encounter; however simple or sophisticated may be the equipment at his disposal. It has been said that 'nothing is impossible in special effects', it is equally true to say that 'nothing is impossible on an animation stand'.

Animation

Only in the simplest forms of animation is each different picture drawn individually. A few animators draw ever-changing shapes directly on to film. Also, some simple films can be made by sequentially filming pictures drawn on paper.

Inevitably in this type of animation both the characters and the backgrounds have to be simple so that they can be re-drawn more easily and accurately for each new movement. The background features are copied from one drawing onto the next, but are never quite identical. So that when the entire sequence is filmed, the static features in the background appear to wobble. This totally fluid picture is quite acceptable as long as it keeps wobbling; but if holds are introduced the picture appears to 'freeze' for the duration of the hold. Alternately shooting two or three copies of the static scene gives the hold the same wobble as the moving scenes.

Cel animation

Animated characters are normally painted on clear acetate cels so that they can be filmed against one drawing of the background for each scene. The background can then be a good, detailed painting. This is usually done on strong paper which has been stretched so that it does not buckle. Parts of the background may also be painted on cels, so that the characters can go behind them.

Several cels can be used at the same time so that the different elements of animation can move in different ways. The cels and the background are located exactly in the required position by specially designed registration pegs on the camera table.

If more than one animated character is used, then each one can be drawn separately on a separate series of cels so that their movements can be totally independent. In the same way, parts of a figure can be broken down and drawn on different cel layers to avoid unnecessary re-drawing of those parts of the figure which remain static or move slowly. The cels are carefully marked so that the cameraman can identify them immediately.

The separation into layers does not follow any hard and fast rule – it depends largely on the subject. Two characters in the same scene may be tackled on separate cels in one instance; and in another they can be split between the layers in such a way that each layer carries a part of both characters.

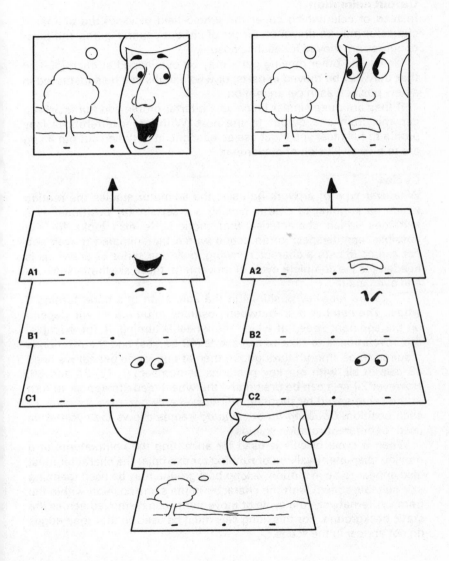

CEL ANIMATION

The background and the basic cel of the face remain the same.
Other features, on separate cels, can be used in different combinations to give
different expressions to the character.

Cutout Animation Movement Cycles

Cutout animation
Instead of cels (which cover the whole field of view) the animated character may be drawn on pieces of cut out paper. Figures and parts of figures are moved for each exposure.

Limbs and other moving parts may be overlapped at each joint so that they can be moved in parts; or whole limbs can be substituted in a new position as in cel animation.

If they are quite similar (such as a quarter profile and full face) you can mix from one cutout to the next. With larger differences (say profile to full face) you must use at least one in-between cut out if you are to give an illusion of movement.

Cycles
Whatever type of artwork he uses, the animator studies the motion which he is going to create, picking out certain *key* positions – i.e. extremes which characterise that motion. He also looks for the possible repetitiveness of an action within the animated movement. For example, with a character rowing, only one series of drawings is needed for the complete cycle of movement; these are then used over and over again.

There are four key positions in the animation of a hand turning a wheel. The number of in-between positions to be drawn will depend on the apparent speed at which the wheel is turning. If, for example, one revolution is to take two seconds (48 frames) and the rotation is required to be smooth throughout, then at one frame per cel we need 48 cels in all, with our key positions at numbers 1, 12, 24 and 36. However 24 cels can be drawn and the wheel made to appear to turn at the same speed by shooting *on twos* – i.e. two frames are taken of each position. *Doubling up* or *skipping* frames allows the cycle to be used for different rotation speeds.

When a cycle of cels is used for animating the components of a moving character (walking or running for example) the character must also appear to be in motion. A long background may be used (panning at a suitable speed) with the character in the same position within the frame. Alternatively, the cycle of movements can be moved across the static background. For this, long cels must be used so that their edges do not appear in the scene.

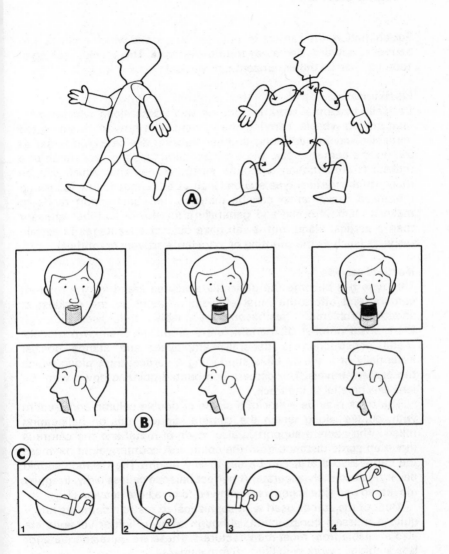

CUT-OUTS AND CYCLES

A. **Breakdown of a cutout character**
   Each component can be moved independently, or substituted by an alternative one.

B. The character's mouth or jaw can be cut-out and moved in sync with a voice.

C. **Cycles**
   Movement is broken down to key positions. A set of cels or cutouts can be used to repeat movements again and again.

13

The Stand

For animation, the camera is mounted on a stand which enables it to be moved towards and away from the artwork. This travel (tracking or zooming) can be either horizontal or vertical.

Horizontal stands

Basically horizontal work is done on two tracks along which runs a platform on wheels, carrying the camera. The artwork is supported vertically and moved along another tracking device which is set at 90° to the camera track. Most horizontal stands are very much of a makeshift construction; although all the refinements which can be found on the vertical type stands (such as automatic follow focus and motorised movements) can be installed. Its construction tends to make it clumsy to use and generally a lot slower and less efficient than a vertical stand; but it can have distinct advantages in certain respects (such as the shooting of extra large artwork or models).

Vertical stands

This type has become the generally accepted stand for the rostrum camera, and offers the most efficient solutions to the trickiest of shooting problems. It has become reasonably standardised, although there are a number of manufacturers producing their own models. Metal construction is generally employed, and stands consist essentially of a square base supporting a vertical track along which the camera travels. The camera is mounted pointing down with the lens axis parallel to the track.

The track may be either of a single or double column constructim with 'guides' along which the camera support runs on ballbearing rollers. The camera support is also made of metal and the camra is mounted some distance from the column. A counterweight balances the camera so that it can be set to any height. The balance should never be absolutely accurate. A perfect balance causes jerky, irregular moves, so one side is generally allowed to be a little heavier.

Most of the stands used with sophisticated rostrum cameras are of quite a massive construction; although smaller, lighter versions are also available from most manufacturers. These are quite adequate for less ambitious work with light 16 mm cameras.

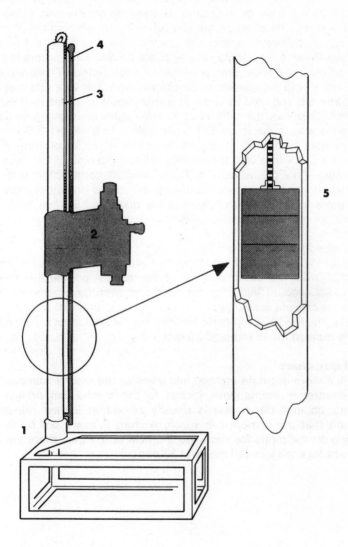

SINGLE COLUMN STAND

1, Column and base. 2, Camera mount and camera. 3, Chain drive. 4, Follow focus rack. 5, Counter weight inside column.

Tracking and Field Size

The camera is normally moved up and down (tracked) by a motor located at the base of the stand. Depending on the lens fitted, the camera height determines the size of the area photographed – *the field size.* A calibrated wheel and a mechanical counter at the front of the base allow for accurate setting of the height. The camera may be tracked during a shot. This produces a zoom effect. The counter is essential in the calculation of smooth zooms. For example, assume the camera is required to zoom in continuously from one field size to another. Suppose the difference between the counter readings for two sizes was found to be 1500, and the zoom is to last 150 frames. The camera is moved 10 points for each frame of picture. If the division results in a less convenient number (like say 11½) then the calibrations on the wheel itself are used in conjunction with the counter. It must be remembered that the digits on the counter are only there to aid the calculations of the distance between field sizes and do not represent specific units of measure.

Field size indicator

A useful visual aid to the cameraman is a strip of wood (or similar material) mounted along the side of the track. A pointer attached to the camera mount indicates the field size seen by a particular lens when the camera uses only one lens and one gauge. For a dual gauge camera, the field size indicator has to carry two columns for each lens clearly marked for 16 mm and 35 mm.

Field size chart

This is a more accurate method and involves the mechanical counter. The counter is permanently locked to the mechanism driving the camera up and down and is usually zeroed at lowest maximum position that the camera can reach. A chart is made out by simply reading off the digits for each specific field size. Again there are two columns for each lens (16 mm and 35 mm).

Double column stand
1, Columns and base. 2, Camera mount and camera. 3, Chain drives. 4, Counter weight. 5, Field size indicator in position.

35 mm		16 mm	
55mm	28mm	55mm	28mm

Field size indicator

	35mm		16mm	
FS	55mm	28mm	55mm	28mm
1″				
2″				
3″				
4″				

Field size chart

17

Artwork Table

In its simplest form this can be just a table, a support on which the artwork to be photographed is placed or held. Static shots involving cel changes only and some types of cutout animation are possible with such a set-up.

The platen

A piece of artwork can be stuck down to the table, but this is not a very good idea as the heat from the lights tends to make it crinkle up. So a piece of glass – the platen – is introduced to keep the artwork flat at all times. It must be free of any optical distortions and great care must be taken in the way it is positioned over the artwork to make sure that the pressure is correct each time.

If the pressure of the glass platen is insufficient, the artwork can buckle in places; if cels are used, then the upper layers will throw shadows on the background – and each time the glass is lifted off (to change cels) the shape of the shadow may change, resulting in a flicker which can be very noticeable. If, on the other hand, the pressure is too great, this will produce Newton's Rings on the cels. The platen glass is normally fitted into a metal frame attached to the rostrum table. The frame can be adjusted to ensure even pressure over the whole area of the glass and to take different thicknesses of artwork.

Adjusting the platen

When the platen is 'lying flat on the table' it should not in fact be in contact with the table. Adjustment can be checked by sliding a flat piece of paper between the platen glass and the rostrum table and making sure that it has equally free movement on all sides.

When the platen is lifted up it is automatically locked in that position, leaving the cameraman with both hands free to change the artwork. A twist of the handle releases the lock and the platen can be lowered again.

Padding

To make sure that the different cel layers and the background are pressed together so that no shadows are visible, you must use 'padding', such as soft tissue paper crumpled up behind the background.

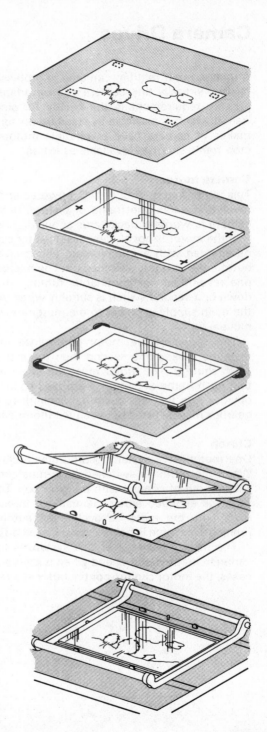

Simple table
The artwork can be stuck down with double-sided tape.

Loose glass
A piece of glass may be placed on the artwork. Use register marks to make sure it always goes down in the same place.

Spacers
Coins or similar spacers may be used to raise glass so that it holds but does not press on the artwork.

The Platten
The platten is a piece of plain glass hinged to the table. When it is down, it should hold the artwork without pressing on it too hard.

Camera Drives

Although most rostrum cameras in professional use are of a special design, virtually any camera can be adapted for this purpose. The primary requirement is the facility for single-frame shooting (stop frame) which is available as standard on some 16 mm cameras. Most makes of camera have compatible motors, especially designed for stop-frame shooting, available as extras.

Camera motor

This motor can be A.C. or D.C. powered and is connected so that one revolution takes one frame of picture. It must be able to drive the camera forwards or backwards at one or more 'constant' speeds.

If the motor is not already designed for single-frame shooting it can be adapted with a suitable cam and microswitch. At the touch of a button, the motor is switched on. The microswitch stops it again after one revolution. For continuous running the button is kept pressed down or a second switch is suitably wired. A separate switch controls the main supply of power to the motor and selects forward or reverse movement.

The speed of the motor determines the exposure time; if one revolution takes one second then the exposure time is $\frac{1}{2}$ sec. (with 180° shutter). The motor must run at an exactly constant speed so that each frame of picture is exposed equally (a flickering effect is an obvious sign that this is not happening). To vary the exposure time, a gearbox may be fitted between the motor and the camera.

Clutch

One motor drive system incorporates a clutch as well as a gearbox. When the motor is switched on it runs continuously, but the clutch keeps it out of contact with the gear box. To operate the camera, the clutch is engaged either manually or through a solenoid. After one revolution, the motor is declutched automatically. For continuous running the clutch is held in the engaged position as long as required.

The main advantage of this system is that it eliminates possible variation in the motor speed when it is stopping and starting. In some cases, the motor can run continuously at a range of speeds.

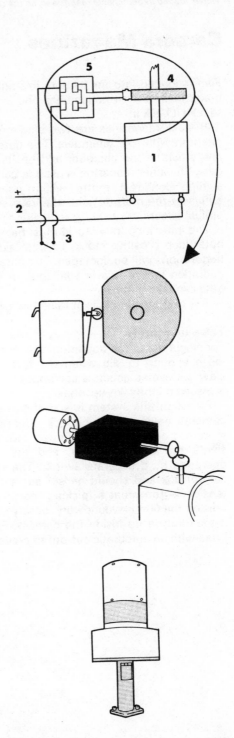

Simplified wiring for stop-motion operation
1, Motor. 2, Power supply. 3, Start button. 4, Cam. 5, Contact breaker. When the start button is pressed, this overrides the contact breaker, and allows the motor to revolve. Unless the button is held down, the motor stops after one revolution.

Geared motor
A gearbox between the motor and the camera gives control over camera speeds with a constant motor speed.

Printed circuit motor
This type of motor is used to give a selection of speeds. It can perform all the stopping, starting, and other control functions without any further circuitry.

21

Camera Magazines

Film is loaded into the camera in single or bi-pack magazine. Single magazines have two chambers, one to feed the film out and the other to take it back in.

Bi-pack magazines are two single magazines joined together into one unit with four chambers. The outer magazine carries unexposed raw stock in one chamber and on its way to and from the camera gate. The inner magazine is used to carry a positive print of a scene or a high constrast matte which goes through the camera gate *emulsion-to-emulsion* with the raw stock. This is used for various optical effects.

The inner loop (raw stock) must be one perforation shorter than the outer loop (Positive stock) on both sides of the gate, otherwise the perforations will be damaged. The gate should also be set for bi-pack operation where this is available. In practice, virtually any camera gate can take bi-pack.

The best steadiness is obtained at lower camera speeds.

Take-up motors

For single magazine operation, the take-up drive is via a belt which is loose enough to slip when the reel is large and therefore turning slower. Reverse action is accomplished by twisting the belt before it is placed on the take-up wheel

Although this system is sometimes used with bi-pack magazines, cameras equipped for bi-pack operation usually have four torque motors — one for each chamber. Two of these are used for normal single magazine shooting, and the other two are brought into operation by a separate switch. The tension is controlled from the control box and should be set so that it can take a full roll. If the tension is too great a 'picking' noise will be heard. With too little tension the film is wound very loosely on the take-up core. Eventually it may buckle up inside the camera. Fortunately most cameras are fitted with an automatic cut-out to prevent damage if this happens.

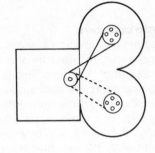

Belt driven single magazine
Twisting the drive belt reverses
the direction of film travel.

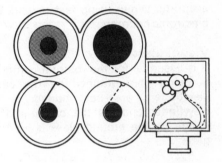

Bipack magazine
Unexposed stock is loaded into
the top chamber of the outer
magazine and taken up by the
bottom chamber of the same
magazine. The inner magazine is
used for positive film in the same
way – loading at the top and take
up at the bottom.

16mm and 35mm sync marks
Stock for bipack filming must be
clearly marked so that all the
components run through the
camera exactly in sync.

Camera Features

Frame counters

Since most animation stand work requires an accuracy to the frame it is preferable to measure the footage going through the camera in frames rather than feet. This is particularly convenient where the dual gauge cameras are concerned. (16 mm and 35 mm conversion tables are at the end of the book.) Both mechanical and electronic counters are used. The mechanical counters are driven directly by the shaft driving the camera. They are essentially more reliable but less conveniently placed. Electronic counters, on the other hand, can be located on the main control console, away from the camera. Any counter must count forward and backward, and stay absolutely accurate. When using fast rewind, beware of possible trip-ups with electronic counters.

Viewfinders

It is essential for the rostrum cameraman to know exactly what area is being photographed by the camera. So, cameras with reflex viewfinders are best suited. A normal *straight-through reflex* viewfinder enables the cameraman to see through the lens. The image on the ground glass is identical to the image in the camera gate.

Rack-over reflex viewfinders also make it possible for the cameraman to see through the lens. For viewing, the camera is racked over so that the ground glass in the viewfinder is opposite the lens. It is in exactly the same position as the camera gate during shooting. A trip-switch is usually installed so that the camera cannot operate until it is racked back to the shooting position. The only disadvantage of this system is that it is not possible to look through while shooting (racking over in the middle of a shot is not advisable and should only be resorted to when it is absolutely unavoidable).

The Rostrum Cameraman does not look through the camera when he is actually shooting. The viewfinder is only used for lining up before he starts shooting, so there is really little disadvantage to the rack-over type of viewfinder.

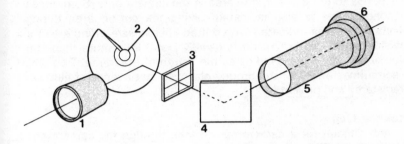

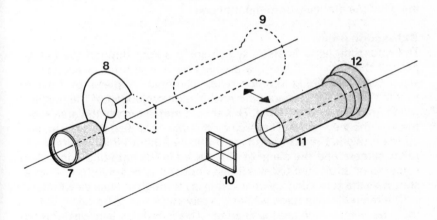

VIEWFINDERS

Reflex viewfinder
The cameraman can either look through the reflex system at the scene he is
shooting, or shine a light through it and line up to the projected image of the gate
aperture.

Rack-over reflex viewfinder
Rackover can be motorised and operated from the control console. 1, Camera lens.
2, Shutter. 3, Graticule. 4, Mirror. 5, Viewfinder. 6, Eyepiece. 7, Camera lens. 8,
Shutter. 9, Viewing position. 10, Graticule. 11, Viewfinder. 12, Eyepiece.

Viewfinder Details

Ground glass graticule

The ground glass in the viewfinder has a graticule engraved on it. This corresponds to the actual frame area in the camera gate. Sometimes a secondary line is also indicated, giving the cut-off area during projection. An area indicated with dotted lines is *safe titling* area for television, although the cut-off is usually just a little more than film projector cut off. A cross indicates the centre of the frame. Two pins are sometimes built into the ground glass, so that a piece of film can be registered and projected.

Rotoscope lamp

It is very difficult for a cameraman to look through the camera and move the artwork to get the desired framing; in fact, it is often made a physical impossibility by the distance between the camera and the artwork. To get over this problem and speed up the process of lining up, a lamp is attached to the viewfinder. The light projects a sharp image of the graticule onto the artwork.

Rotoscope prism

The rotoscope lamp is also used to shine a light through the actual gate of the camera through a prism. This is useful for checking the viewfinder and lining up non-reflex cameras. A piece of frosted viewing film in the camera gate enables the projection of the full film frame onto the rostrum table. This should match exactly the area seen through the viewfinder. The projected image may also be used to line up the artwork. If a standard type graticule is photographed first on a reflex camera and the piece of film placed in the gate of a non-reflex camera and projected (as described above) it is possible to line up a shot with the same degree of accuracy as through a reflex viewfinder.

The main disadvantage is that the raw stock has to be taken out of the gate before each shot is lined up. This is tedious and wasteful on stock, because the camera has to be run on each time to prevent fogging of the preceeding take. So external references on a pantograph table are normally used to get over this problem. (see p. 54).

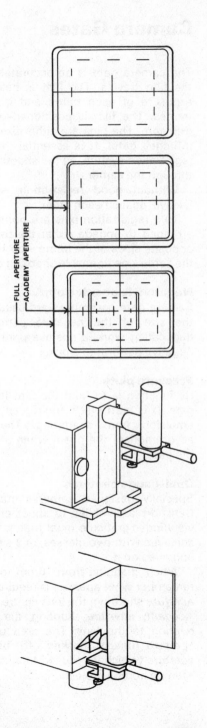

16mm graticule

35mm graticule
Showing full and academy
apertures.

FULL APERTURE
ACADEMY APERTURE

16 and 35mm graticule

Rotoscope Lamp
Rotoscope lamp mounted for
projecting through the viewfinder.

Rotoscope lamp mounted for
projecting through the camera
gate via a prism.

27

Camera Gates

The camera gate is an accurately machined aperture behind which the film travels. The film is held exactly steady during the actual exposure of each frame and is moved on intermittently between frames. The film is positioned on registration (pilot) pins for each exposure. The pins are either fixed (Bell and Howell gate) or moving (Mitchell gate). It is essential that the camera should have a good registration system, as the shooting often involves more than one run through the camera.

Without good registration, separately shot elements tend to 'weave' against each other.

Two registration pins are normally employed. On 35mm they are arranged to engage either the top or bottom pair of perforations on opposite sides of the frame – on 16mm the two pins are positioned on the same side to enable shooting on single-perforated stock.

Negative & positive pins
Camera gate assemblies are usually fitted with pins compatible with the size of the negative perforations (Neg. Pins). For bi-pack duplicating work, a positive print can be made by the laboratory on negative perforated stock.

Pressure plate
Its function is to hold the film flat, and exactly in contact with the gate. It is matt black, to stop any light that may go through the film emulsion from scattering. The pressure plate is removed to accommodate the prism when a piece of film is rotoscoped through the gate.

Dual-gauge cameras
Specially designed cameras may have interchangeable gate and transport assemblies to shoot either on 16mm or 35mm film. The viewfinder graticule must match the appropriate gauge. This can be achieved with two glasses, or a single glass which has both graticules engraved on it.

When changing from 16mm to 35mm shooting, it is important to remember what aperture is required: full aperture or Academy. For *full aperture* shooting, the lens centre remains the same as for 16mm. For *Academy aperture* shooting, the camera body has to be moved in relation to the lens. The area photographed may still be the full aperture (unless masked off); but only the area of the Academy aperture (which is reduced to accommodate an optical soundtrack) is seen on normal projection.

CAMERA GATES

Moving the film through the camera

The film is transported through the camera body by a transport mechanism (1). It is exposed at the camera gate (2).

Interchangeable assemblies

1, Transport assembly.
2, Gate assembly.

Registration systems

Fixed pins registration.

Moving pins registration.

Registration points on 35mm and 16mm.

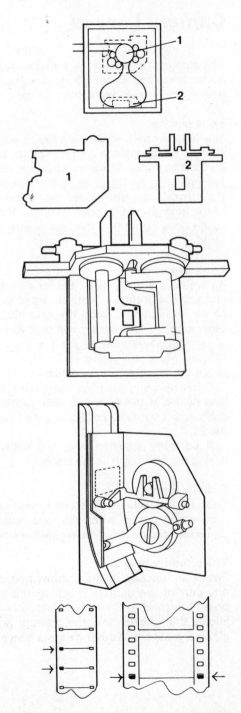

Camera Lenses

The standard lenses for 16 mm shooting are 28mm – 32mm, and for 35mm shooting 50mm – 55mm, although lenses of virtually any focal length can be used with either gauge.

Lens centre

The lens centre should normally match the centre of the field being shot. If, for example, a lens is lined up to shoot full aperture it can still be used to shoot Academy aperture, because this area is covered by the lens anyway. However, if the camera were to track in (zoom in) on the artwork, the lens centre would stay in the same place regardless of the field-size being photographed. Since the centre of the Academy frame does not match the lens centre the final result has a sideways 'drift'.

Lens alignment

As we have already seen, the lens centre should be indicated by the cross on the graticule in the centre of the frame. The lens axis has also to be in alignment with the axis along which the camera travels, otherwise the lens centre will drift when tracking. Provided there are no serious imperfections on the track, the lens can be aligned as follows. Mark the projected lens centre at a chosen field size, then move the camera to a field size which is *double the first, plus one* (if the first field size was 3in, then the second would be 7in); Mark the lens centre at this field size also; loosen up the lens on its mounting and reset it with the centre at a half-way position between your two marks.

If correctly adjusted, the lens centre should not drift or weave during the full length of the track.

Coaxial lens

This is a specially designed lens which makes a deliberate use of the drift, which occurs when the lens centre is misaligned. A zoom and pan effect can be achieved by deliberately displacing the lens centre.

The shadow board

The main function of the shadow board is to prevent reflection from any part of the camera reaching the artwork. It is a black-painted board attached to the camera mount. An aperture in the middle of it allows the lens to 'see' the artwork and is used for carrying ripple glasses, masks, and other gadgets (see p126).

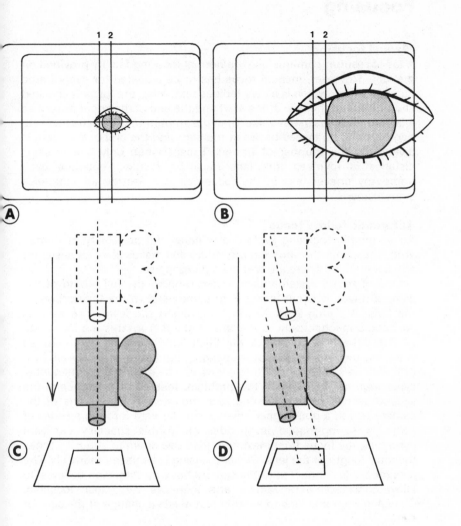

LENS ALIGNMENT

Aperture centres
A. The lens centre should *not* be aligned with full aperture centre (1) while the artwork is placed in the academy aperture centre (2).
B. If it is, you will get a sideways drift away from the lens centre on zooming in.

Line to travel
C. When the lens axis is parallel to the axis along which the camera travels, the lens centre will stay at the same position throughout the full length of the zoom.
D. When the lens axis is not parallel to the axis of travel, the lens centre will drift during the zoom. The extent of this drift is proportional to the degree of misalignment.

Focusing

Manual focusing

A lot of rostrum cameras use the normal focusing facility provided on the lens. However, manual focus has to be adjusted for every frame during a zoom, which is a very tedious task. First, the focus is checked and marked on the lens at the start and the end of the zoom as well as a couple of places in between. Then the amount that the lens focusing ring needs to be turned between the start and the end of the zoom is divided by the number of frames. Except when only a very short distance is involved, the lens must be focused between each frame.Any unevenness in the focus-pull can destroy an otherwise smooth zoom.

Automatic follow focus

An automatic focusing system eliminates the possibility of human error, speeds up the shooting procedure and makes life a lot easier for the cameraman. There are two main types in use.

One of these systems uses a cam running the full length of the camera travel. It is cut (shaped) to correspond to the focus curve of the lens. A spring-loaded lever rides along this cam. The lever is connected mechanically to the lens, and either rotates the focus ring or slides the lens up and down. Each lens needs its own cam, so changing the lens necessitates changing the entire cam as well. Two or three cams each for a different lens, can be mounted (permanently) close together to alleviate this problem. Instead of a long cam, the second system uses a toothed rack mounted along the line of the camera travel; a pinion gear drives a circular cam through a series of gears. A spring-loaded lever rides along this specially cut cam controling the focus from maximum field size down to about $1\frac{1}{2}$ times the focal length of the lens. Closer focusing is achieved manually. The lens mount is connected to the camera body by extension bellows, to allow considerable movement and therefore very close focusing. Changing from one lens to another just needs a change of the circular cam.

The focusing plane can be raised or lowered by moving the rack; this way very thick 'artwork' (such as a book, or a model) can be photographed with ease. The lens stays in focus with the focusing plane regardless of where this plane is positioned; the lens focus must be set at zero position. Once focused manually at one field size (by adjusting the rack) the lens will be in focus at other field sizes.

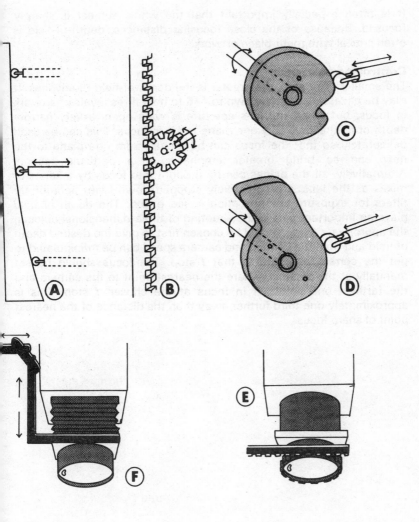

AUTOMATIC FOCUSING

A. Follow-focus cam running full length of the camera travel.
B. Rack and gear for rotating cam system.
C. Auto-focus cam (rotates anticlockwise when zooming in).
D. Inverted auto-focus cam (rotates clockwise when zooming in).
E. Auto-focus drive for normal rotary focusing.
F. Auto-focus drive for lens with bellows focusing.

33

Depth of Field

It is often especially important that the whole subject is sharply focused. Because of the close focusing distances, depth-of-field is often critical with multi-plane artwork.

Controlling sharpness

The smaller the *f* stop, the greater is the depth-of-field of any lens. It may be necessary to stop down to *f* 16 to hold three levels of artwork in focus; but when the lens aperture is wide open, a very narrow depth of field allows only one plane to be in focus. This can be used deliberately so that the focus can be moved from one plane to the next and so bring greater emphasis to a particular action. Alternatively, all the planes can be brought into focus by a series of mixes as the lens is progressively stopped down (with appropriate filters for exposure compensation – see p. 98). The depth of field plays an important part in the shooting of three-dimensional objects; the appropriate *f* stop should be chosen first to give the desired depth of field and then the lighting and camera speed can be manipulated to get the correct exposure at that *f* stop. The focus should be set manually at the distance where the nearest point to the camera and the farthest one are both in focus at the chosen *f* stop. This is approximately one third further away than the distance of the nearest point of sharp focus.

Focus calibrations
Automatic follow-focus systems
have a manual override which
enable going 'out of focus'
deliberately at any point along the
track. A counter is used to show
the distance from central 'in
focus' position.

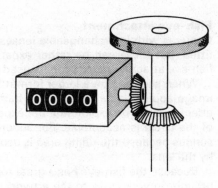

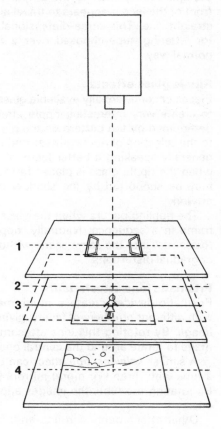

Multiplane artwork
If the primary focus of the lens is
at plane 1, at a large f stop planes
3 and 4 appear out of focus.
When the focus is moved to plane
3, plane 1 and 4 are out of focus.
Reduce the aperture to increase
depth-of-field, greatest coverage
is given when focused on 2.

Optical Effects

Fish-eye attachment

Cameras with interchangeable lenses can have a proper fish-eye lens fitted, but these can be rather expensive and their use is limited. A fish-eye attachment lens can be used to convert the standard lens.

When shooting on a larger format than the lens is intended for, the image appears as a circle in the frame; this in itself is an interesting effect and can be exploited if the exposure drop-out around the edges of the circle is acceptable. For superimpositions this handicap is not serious because the titling area is usually well within the area covered by the lens.

Because the fish-eye has a great focusing range, the camera can be brought in very close to the artwork. When the artwork is panned in front of the lens it appears to travel along a spherical path instead of a straight one. This three-dimensional illusion is particularly effective for lettering superimposed over a flat scene photographed in the normal way.

Ripple glass effects

Pieces of commercially available glass of various patterns can be used to create very interesting ripple effects. The pattern of the ripple is determined by the pattern on the glass. Special care should be given to the selection of ripple glasses and the focussing of the camera lens; generally speaking a better focus of the distorted image is achieved when the ripple glass is placed farther away from the lens. The glass may be supported by the shadow board, or placed just above the artwork.

The rippling occurs when the glass is moved slightly between each frame in a sequence. Naturally, ripple effects can be *cut* or *mixed (dissolved)* into the same scene without ripple to create either sudden or gradual distortions.

Prismatic lens attachments

Prismatic devices create a multi-image effect and can be obtained with different numbers of facets, giving different multiplications of the image. By rotating this lens attachment the multiple images can be made to rotate around the central one.

A similar *kaleidoscope* effect can be obtained by shooting through a tube with three (or more) mirrors (front-silvered mirrors are ideal). By rotating the tube, the images appear to rotate around the central one.

Other attachments can flop an image, rotate it around the axis of the lens, or reverse it laterally. Similar effects can also be produced with home-made gadgets using mirrors.

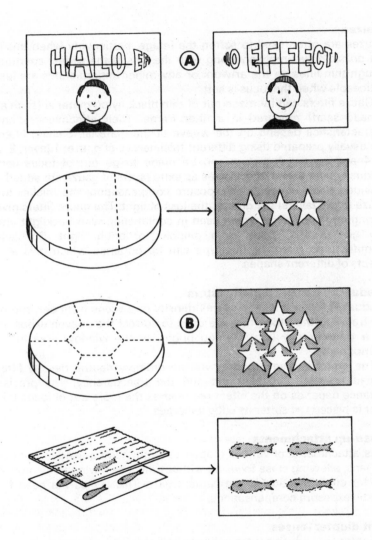

FRONT-OF-LENS ATTACHMENTS

A. Fish-eye attachment
At very close range you can produce a convex effect with normal artwork. If the artwork is panned E/W the lettering appears to move along a halo-like shape, getting progressively bigger at the centre position and diminishing at the edges.

B. Effect prisms
Prismatic lenses can break up the image or distort it. Even patterned window glasses can be used.

Special Effects Attachments

Gauzes

Gauzes are often used to soften the image, particularly when this is not possible by simply shooting with the lens at the widest aperture. Rough thin lines on the artwork or any minor imperfections are less noticeable when the focus is soft.

Gauze filters can be made out of thin black nylon material (such as a head scarf) mounted in a filter frame. Their effectiveness and characteristics depend on the weave of the material. Several filters are usually prepared using different thicknesses of gauze: 1 layer, 2, 3 or 4 and so on. A picture can be made to go out of focus very gradually by a series of dissolves as extra layers of gauze are added – provided there is adequate exposure compensation; the thicker the gauze (more layers) the greater the loss of light. The gauze filters give a fringing (halo) effect when used in conjunction with backlight and can give a star shape to a pinpoint of bright light. Specially manufactured filters of this type can be obtained which give star effects of different shapes.

Graduated neutral density filters

Graduated filters alter the overall density of a scene from one end of the frame to the other; they are used to correct the uneven exposure on a transparency (e.g. sky too bright, or the window area in an interior shot).

The effect is also possible with an ordinary neutral density filter placed between the backlight and the transparency. The precise distance depends on the effect required as the more out of focus this filter is placed the softer its edge becomes.

Close-up attachments

Lens attachments of various diopter strength can be used in front of the lens, allowing close focusing without the lens having to be moved too far out in relation to the camera gate. This avoids the need for drastic exposure compensations.

Split diopter lenses

A diopter lens which covers only one half of the frame allows close up focusing in that area while the rest of the frame is unaffected. This way an object attached to the shadow board (and lit separately) can be held in focus at the same time as the background artwork on the table.

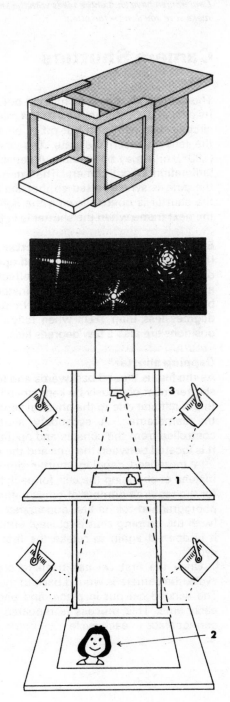

Filter holder
A simple support can carry
several filters if necessary.

Diffusion
Diffusion filters can make dots of
light appear as stars of different
shapes.

Split-focus lens
You can focus artwork both on
the shadow board (1) and on the
table (2) to combine two images.
The split-diopter lens (3) is placed
in front of the camera lens.

Camera Shutters

The camera shutter is positioned between the lens and the film gate. Its design depends on the camera make, but generally speaking it is a circular disc with part cut off to allow the image-forming light from the lens to reach the gate. The open sector may be half the disc (180°), or it may be variable. A variable shutter is useful on a rostrum (animation stand) camera. The intermittent movement of the film in the gate is synchronised so that the film is in a static position when the shutter is open, allowing the light to go through. It moves on to the next frame when the shutter is in the closed position.

Exposure control with the shutter

If a variable shutter is set at a half open position (90°) instead of fully open (180°) the exposure is effectively reduced by one f stop, assuming the camera speed is constant. At a 45° setting it is reduced by one more stop and so on. In reality most shutters are a few degrees less than 180° when fully open, so half- and quarter-open positions are also a few degrees less.

Capping shutter

As the film is wound backwards and forwards through the camera the shutter must obviously be kept closed when not shooting. Sometimes this is difficult due to the physical separation between the camera and the cameraman. A secondary shutter can be installed. This is controlled from the console and operated by a simple solenoid motor. It is located between the lens and the rotary shutter.

A motorised capping shutter simplifies shooting a cycle of cels. Instead of changing the cels for each frame, each cel is photographed for the required number of times before being changed. The first cel is photographed for its first appearance, then the camera is wound on (with the capping shutter closed) until the end of the first cycle. Then it is opened again to retake the first cel at the start of the second cycle.

Once the first cel has been recorded for the beginning of each cycle, the camera is wound back to the second frame of the first cycle. The second cel put in place, and photographed in its correct place each time. This process is repeated until each cel appears at the correct place in each cycle.

Rotary shutter
The sector rotates to reveal the
film aperture. Here set to 180°.

Manual control set at 90°.

Capping shutter
1, Open. 2, Closed.

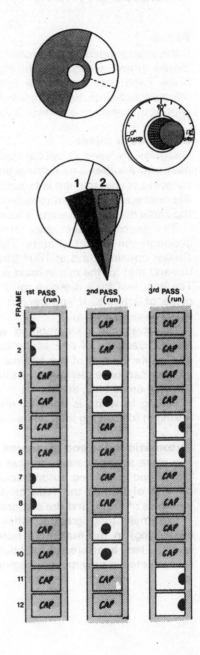

FRAME	1st PASS (run)	2nd PASS (run)	3rd PASS (run)
1	●	CAP	CAP
2	●	CAP	CAP
3	CAP	●	CAP
4	CAP	●	CAP
5	CAP	CAP	●
6	CAP	CAP	●
7	●	CAP	CAP
8	●	CAP	CAP
9	CAP	●	CAP
10	CAP	●	CAP
11	CAP	CAP	●
12	CAP	CAP	●

Shooting a cycle with a capping shutter
Instead of changing the artwork
each frame (or two) the cycle can
be shot in separate passes. The
artwork is changed between
passes. The shutter is opened and
closed for the appropriate passes.
Motorised and automated
capping shutters make this
operation very easy, but it can
also be done manually.

41

Shutter Effects

Fades
If the shutter opening is reduced progressively from fully open to fully closed during a sequence of exposures, it gives a gradual fade to black. Each time the shutter opening is closed a given amount the *effective exposure time* is reduced. However, the time it takes for the shutter to complete one revolution is unaltered.

Dissolves or mixes
Dissolves are used as optical transitions where one scene appears to melt into another. The camera shutter is progressively closed on the outgoing scene; the film is wound back to the start of the dissolve and the new scene is then introduced as the shutter is gradually opened in the same number of frames it took to close it.

The exposure must stay at the same level during a dissolve although the scenes change. This is accomplished only if the total shutter opening stays at 180° throughout. So the opening for the mix out and that for the mix in *must* add up to 180° for every single frame. The best test for a dissolve routine is to mix in and out on the same piece of artwork. If you cannot see the dissolve during projection, then it was successful.

Dissolves can be combined with other effects for sophisticated results. Sections of one scene can be made to dissolve into a new one, while the rest of the original picture remains unchanged; several images can be superimposed either over the full picture area or in selected areas only; and so on.

Fading to white is done by mixing out (dissolving) the scene and mixing in (dissolving in) a white card.

Automatic fades and dissolves
The more sophisticated cameras usually include built-in facilities for fading and dissolving automatically. The cameraman just selects the number of frames the fade or dissolve will take (usually 8, 12, or multiples of them) and the camera does the rest.

Extremely long gradual fades can be achieved by *mixing out* (dissolving) in the maximum number of frames and then *mixing in* with the lens aperture stopped down as desired; as soon as the mix in is completed, a new mix out begins . . . etc.

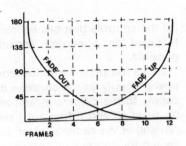

Fade graph
Shutter angle is altered between
180° and 0° from frame to frame.

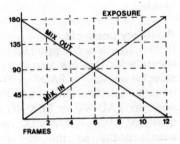

Mix graph
When mixing, the shutter angles
must add up to the same (usually
180°) for each frame.

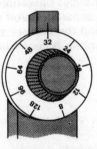

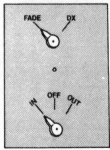

Automatic fades and dissolves
Frame selector for choosing
length of effect.
Control panel.

43

The Control Box

All the controls that can be 'removed' from the camera and stand are installed on a control console from which remote operation is possible.

In its simplest form the console has the main on/off switch for power supply to the console; a separate on/off switch governing the supply to the camera motor; an electronic frame counter (which can be reset to zero); forward / reverse switch for forward and reverse running of the camera motor; button for single frame operation; on/off switch for continuous shooting; camera speed selector; (a foot pedal for single-frame operation can be used to free the cameraman's hands.)

Auxiliary controls

If the camera is equipped with an automatic fade/mix device then the controls for this are also installed on the console. They consist of a selector switch for FADE or DISSOLVE and a second switch marked IN and OUT (FADING or MIXING in – the shutter is closed at the start position; FADING or MIXING OUT – the shutter is open at the start position). The FADE/MIX mechanism is brought into operation automatically as the camera is activated for either single or continuous operation.

A separate on/off switch governs the supply of power to the motor driving the camera assembly up and down the column; the speed of the motor is controlled by a rheostat.

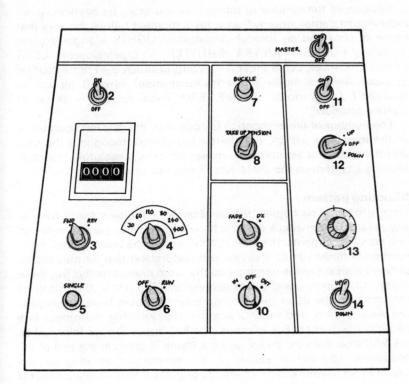

BASIC CONTROL BOX

1, Mains switch. 2, Camera switch (power supply). 3, Forward/reverse switch. 4, Camera speed selector. 5, Single frame button. 6, Off/continuous run. 7, Buckle switch. 8, Take up tension adjustment. 9, Fade/dissolve selector. 10, In/off/out fade or dissolve. 11, Power supply switch. 12, Up/off/down selector. 13, Rheostat control pot (speed). 14, Jog switch – up/down.

Operating the Camera

Manual operation

During the actual shooting all moves are performed by the cameraman turning the control wheel a desired amount for every frame.

Because of the number of things that can easily be overlooked, an experienced cameraman will stop for a moment before the very first frame of shot and go through a checklist: LIGHTS – angle, correct filtration; FOCUS; CAMERA SHUTTER – (open/closed); LENS APERTURE – set; LENS FILTER – in/out; CONSOLE – Frame counter at zero? Camera motor on? Forward-reverse? Mix off (or set as required)? Zoom motor off? N/S; E/W; Zoom rotation – all set at starting position?

The number of times shooting is done with the lens left open wide, or the lens filter left off, the shutter left closed throughout the shot and the focus not set correctly, makes checking absolutely essential. Missing any item on the checklist can ruin the entire shot.

Shooting pattern

Once the shooting begins, the cameraman's troubles aren't over by any means. The chances are that he will be moving the N/S wheel at one set of increments, the E/W at another and the zoom a third; if the rotation is thrown in as well one can understand that he may not be pleased with someone barging into the room unexpectedly! But these things do happen – and the telephone will ring just in the middle of the shot! So the other rule the cameraman should have is a *regular shooting pattern,* and make a point of always doing the moves in a particular sequence. For example, the N/S move always followed by the E/W one, then the zoom, and the frame is taken at the end of the sequence. The actual sequence is unimportant as long as the cameraman always knows where his sequence ends – because that is the only point where he can stop *for whatever reason.* To disregard this rule can lead to some of the moves being made twice, or forgotten . . . the camera taking two frames on the same set up or else missing it altogether.

Errors usually show up at the end of the shot when some of the moves are found to differ from the calculated end positions, (or it can be the camera counter which does not agree with the original calculations). In this case the wisest thing to do is to double check the original calculations, and if these prove right then there is no alternative but to reshoot. Hoping that it may not be noticeable in the rushes is a bad policy; and it's easier to re-shoot while the table is all set up than to have to start from scratch the next day.

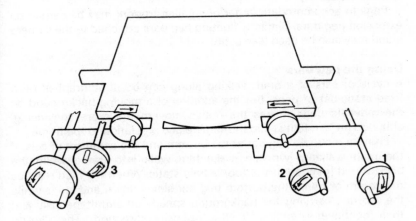

CHECKLIST

LIGHTS
FOCUS
SHUTTER
APERTURE
FILTER

Console

FRAME COUNTER
CAMERA MOTOR
FORWARD / REVERSE
MIX ON/OFF
ZOOM MOTOR ON/OFF
N/S   ROTATION
E/W   ZOOM

OPERATING THE CAMERA

Checklist
Make out a checklist, and follow it before every shot.

Shooting pattern
Label the controls with direction arrows, and *always* operate them in the same sequence.

Registration, Peg Bars

Animation calls for accurate movement. Each piece of artwork is registered on a series of pegs (usually three; a round one with a flat one each side). One edge of each piece of artwork is perforated on a suitable punch, so that they can all be held in register.

Peg-bars

The pegs may be static, but most available animation tables have moving peg bars built in; they run the full length of the table and are connected to a worm-screw drive. As a small wheel at the edge of the table is turned the bar slides backward or forward in its groove. A mechanical counter indicates the distance travelled by the peg bar in 10ths of an inch, and the wheel can be calibrated to measure in 0.001 inch intervals. A set of pegs may be fitted at various positions along each bar.

There is usually more than one movable peg bar on an animation table; they often come in pairs – one at the top and one at the bottom of the picture area, or two at the top and two at the bottom. (Drive wheels and counters are all placed close together along the front edge of the table.)

Pegs to accommodate larger or smaller artwork may be carried on extension peg bars. Similarly floating peg bars attached to the camera stand may also be used (see p. 56).

Using the peg bars

A cycle of cels of a man walking along can be photographed on a fixed static set of pegs, but the addition of a moving background on the movable pegs makes the man's movements more convincing, although he is in fact still in the same place in relation to the frame.

Using a movable peg bar at the bottom and the same set of cels of the man walking, we can make him walk into frame while the background (pegged at the top) is held static. When the man reaches the centre of frame the bottom peg bar slows down and stops while the top one carrying the background speeds up simultaneously and then continues panning in the opposite direction. The illusion achieved this way is that of the camera panning along with the man after he has reached the centre of frame.

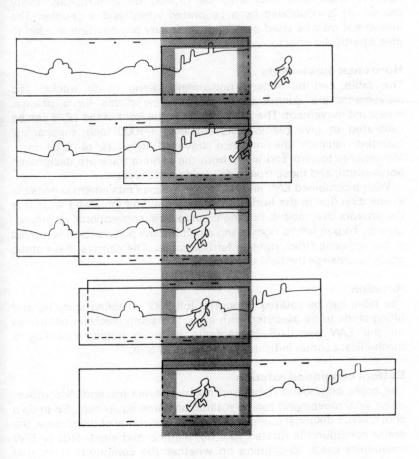

PEG-BAR SHOOTING

The peg-bar lets you move different parts of the scene separately. Here, the man walking (a cycle of cels) is panned west into the scene on the bottom bar. The background (on the top bar) remains stationary until it reaches the centre, then starts to pan east as the bottom bar is stopped.

Movements

Not only can the peg bars move (p48) but so too can the table on its *compound*. It can move horizontally either from side to side, or from back to front, and may also be rotated on a turntable. Every movement is controlled by a calibrated wheel and a counter. The movement may be used separately, or in any combination needed to give a particular effect.

Horizontal movements

The table can be moved horizontally along guide tracks. The movements are connected to worm-screw drives for a precise, measured movement. The drive wheels at the front of the table can be calibrated to give readings as small as 1/1000 inch, mechanical counters indicate the distance travelled in units of 1/10 inch. Movements toward and away from the camera track are designated north-south; and those from side to side, east-west.

With a combined E/W and N/S travel, precise movement is possible in any direction in the horizontal plane. In animation stand work it is the artwork that moves, not the camera as in conventional cinematography. To pan left to right along a picture, the picture itself is moved in the opposite (from right to left) direction. The camera stays static except to change the field size (zoom).

Rotation

The table can be rotated through a full 360° enabling spinning and tilting shots to be executed with ease. The same precision control as on the E/W and N/S movements is incorporated; including a mechanical counter indicating the degree of turn.

Bottom compound rotation

The entire compound (table and pegbars, table rotation, N/S movement, E/W movement) can be rotated on some equipment. So to do a shot using a diagonal move at 30° to the horizontal of the picture, the entire compound is rotated to a 30° setting and either N/S or E/W movement used. (depending on whether the compound is rotated clockwise or counterclockwise).

Inevitably the bottom rotation is of a heavy construction. It is intended to facilitate diagonal pans using only one movement instead of two, and not for rotation during the actual shooting.

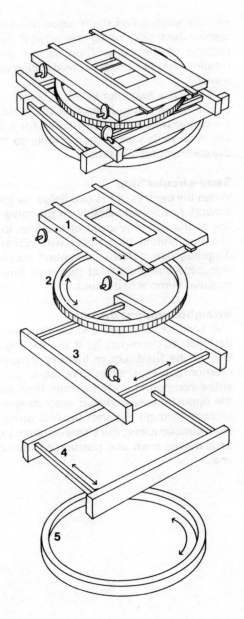

The compound lets you position
the artwork exactly right for each
frame.

Rostrum compound
1, Table top. 2, Table rotation. 3,
N.S. Assembly. 4, E.W. Assembly.
5, Bottom compound rotation.

Using Rotations

For any shots using the rotation movement, extreme care should be taken when positioning the artwork with respect to the centre of rotation of the table. There is not always a simple solution to a rotation shot but careful consideration of the problem will always find a way.

When the two frames are symmetrical lines are drawn from the centre of each frame (parallel to its sides). The point at which they cross gives the centre of rotation for a normal full loop rotation shot. The artwork is placed on the table so that this point corresponds to the centre of table rotation.

Semi-circular loop

When the centres of the two fields are joined by a straight line and the artwork positioned suitably on the table so that the centre of rotation lies at the half way point of this line; this gives a semi-circular loop. The line should be parallel with either N/S or E/W movement (if diagonal, use bottom compound rotation). The artwork is panned along the straight line at the same time as the rotation through the required number of degrees.

Straightening out the loop

The semi-circular loop can be straightened out as required (or even flattened out completely) if the second compound move is used (at 90° to the first). Up to halfway through the shot the semi-circular rotation curve using an E/W move can be modified by moving the entire compound north or south (one way flattens out the curve and the opposite way makes it even steeper!) After this point is reached halfway through the shot the N/S move is equal to the radius of the semi circular curve, the frame appears to rotate around its own centre as it moves from one position to the next along a perfectly straight line.

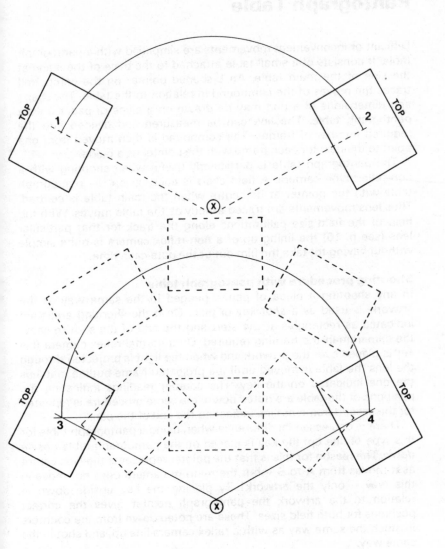

ROTATIONS

If the artwork is positioned so that point X is in the centre of table rotation, a move
from position 1 to position 2 can be accomplished by using rotation only; the result
is a very smooth move. In any other position on the table, the execution of this
move would inevitably require the use of both E/W and N/S movements and would
be extremely difficult to get a really smooth result.

Semi–circular rotation

By using N.S. move as well as the E.W. during the rotation, a semi-circular curve
can be modified – even flattened out into a straight line!

53

Pantograph Table

Difficult or inconvenient movements are simplified with a pantograph table. It consists of a small table attached to the base of the stand at the side of the main table. An L-shaped pointer on the compound traces the moves of the compound in relation to the table. The shape and dimensions of a pan may be drawn on a piece of paper on the pantograph table. The line can be measured and divided into the required number of frames. The compound is then moved from one point to the next for each frame with the pointer as a guide.

The pantograph table is particularly useful when shooting with a non-reflex type camera. A field chart is lined up on the pantograph table with the pointer at its centre when the main table is centred. Thus lens movements are traced exactly as the table moves. With the help of the field-size calibrations along the track for that particular lens (see p. 16) the lining up of a non-reflex camera is quite simple without having tot take the film out ot the gate each time.

Shooting procedure with pantograph table

In any shooting a piece of paper, pegged in the same way as the artwork, is used as a *shot key* or plan. On it the shooting areas are indicated as rectangles at the start and the end of the shot to show the cameraman the framing required. On a normal reflex camera this *key* is placed over the artwork and when the light is projected through the lens the table is moved until the projected frame outline matches the one indicated on the key. The counter readings indicating the positions of the table are noted down; the same procedure is repeated for the second frame outline indicating the end of the pan.

There is one essential difference when using a pantograph table for this type of line up: the key is placed on the pantograph table *upside down*. The reason for this is that the pointer represents the lens centre as it moves from A to B – but the rostrum camera does not move in this way – only the artwork! By placing the key upside down in relation to the artwork the pantograph pointer gives the correct positions for both field sizes. These are noted down from the counters in much the same way as with a reflex camera line up, and shot in the same way.

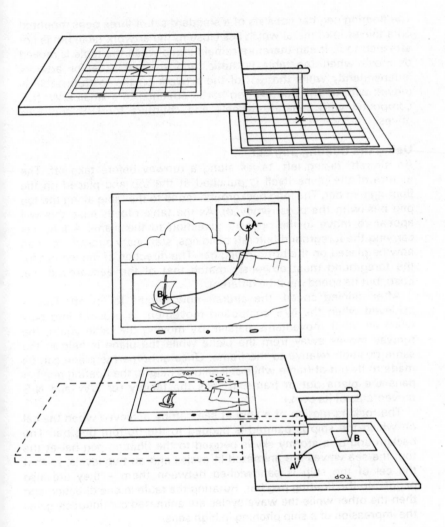

THE PANTOGRAPH TABLE

Rostrum table and pantograph table with pointer.
Artwork with shot key overlayed showing a curved move from field A to field B.

Operating the pantograph
The artwork is placed on the rostrum table the right way up but the shot key is
placed upside down on the pantograph table.

55

Floating Peg Bar

The floating peg bar consists of a standard set of three pegs mounted on a thin strip of metal which lies close to the artwork table but is not attached to it. It can therefore remain static when the table is moved or move when the table is static, and so hold a cel or artwork independently while the rest of the artwork on the rostrum table is moved with it. The floating peg bar is attached to a small E/W; N/S compound with separate wheels and counters for N/S and E/W drives.

Using the floating peg bar

An aircraft, facing left, taxies along a runway before take off. The picture of the plane itself is punched at the top and placed on the floating peg bar. The long background taped to the table along the top peg bar (with the pegs removed). As the table moves east, this will appear to move in the opposite direction to the plane. A long cel carrying the foreground (aircraft buildings, stationary aircraft etc.) can now be placed on the bottom peg bar. The direction of movement for the foreground must obviously match that of the background (i.e. East), but its speed must be different.

After gaining speed, the aircraft now begins to lift off. This is achieved when the N/S compound movement is brought into play while all other movements persist. By moving the table south, the runway moves away from the plane while the plane is held in the same position relative to the frame. Once airborne the plane can be made to fly out of frame while still gaining height; the floating peg bar pans the plane out of frame. (It has the facility for E/W and N/S movements of its own.)

The rocking motion of a ship at sea can be achieved when the cel on which the ship is painted is pegged to the bottom peg bar. The background of a stormy sky is pegged to the floating peg bar at the top; the sea waves are animated in cycles and on two levels, so that the cel of the ship is sandwiched between them — they are also pegged to the floating peg bar. Rotating the table in one direction and then the other while the wave cycles are animated continuously gives the impression of a ship pitching in high seas.

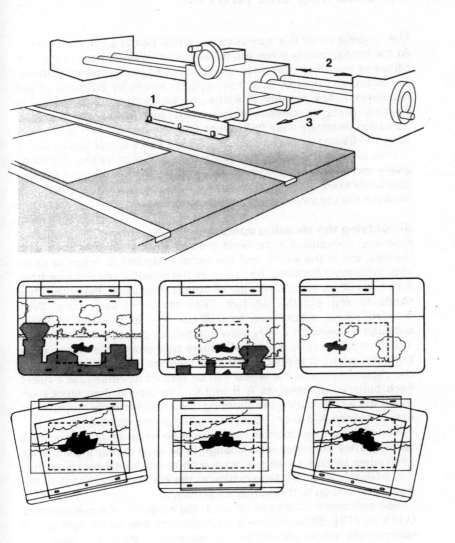

FLOATING PEG-BARS

The equipment
1, The pegbar. 2, E/W movement. 3, N/S movement.
Floating peg bars allow cels to be moved independently. The aeroplane cels are
panned away from the airport background on the floating peg-bars.
Sea and sky background can be held steady on the floating peg-bar and cycle
of waves animated while the table compound is used to rock a storm-tossed ship.

Calculating the Moves

The simplest move is a horizontal or vertical pan at a constant speed. At the shot planning stage the distance is measured from one frame centre to the other. The distance is converted to counter revolutions. For example, 5 inches is 500 revolutions (made by 50 turns of the handwheel). Any number of frames by which this number is easily divisible gives a convenient increment and makes the shooting operation relatively easy (50 frames would mean 0.1 in – one wheel turn; 100 frames would be done at 0.05 in – half a wheel turn etc.)

Very often it is possible to change the number of frames slightly to give a convenient increment. In cases where the number of frames is absolutely fixed, a manipulation of the field size can alter the distance between the centres to a more convenient figure.

Simplifying the shooting operation

However, convenient increments are not always possible even with the best will in the world, and the cameraman has to resort to other aids. With most fractions, he can mark the wheel. If the distance from A to B was 2 in. and the number of frames fixed at 60, the wheel thus needs turning exactly 1/3 turn (0.33 recurring) each time. With detailed wheel calibrations to 0.001 in. this is possible to shoot although it would be a very slow and painful process. The easy way around this is to wind a piece of camera tape around the wheel, mark the point where it overlaps, and then take the tape off again so that the circumference of the wheel can be divided by three (use a ruler). Each point is identified as A B and C. The tape is then stuck back round the wheel; during the shooting the wheel is simply moved in an easy sequence A-B-C or C-B-A, depending on the direction of travel.

The digits on the counter should only be relied upon for the main reading. They are not precise enough to be used during the shooting. Even when shooting a simple move such as one wheel-turn per frame it is advisable to stick a tape marker at the start position and then this marker is lined up to the pointer each time.

Any common fraction can be set. If the incremental move comes to 0.125 in. ($12\frac{1}{2}$ digits, which is equivalent to one wheel-turn plus a quarter) the wheel should be divided in four parts and each part numbered A,B,C,D; during the shooting the cameraman would follow a cycle of: A to A plus B; B to B plus C; C to C plus D; D to D plus A etc.

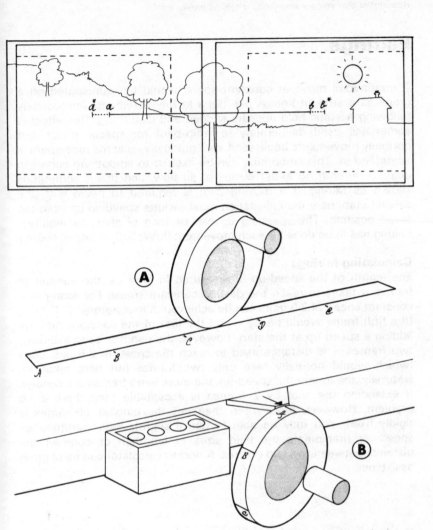

CALCULATING PANS

Adjusting to get a suitable pan length
By reducing the start and end field sizes (a,b) the physical length of the pan has
been extended (a*,b*) to make it more easily divisible by the number of frames (the
length of the pan in time).

Making the pan wheel
Tape can be used to divide circumference of the control wheel. Each segment is
identified by a letter. The wheel calibrations are lined up to a pointer, so fractions of
a turn can be accurately set frame after frame.

Fairings

A continuous move at constant speed would be represented on a graph as a straight line. A pan done at full increments immediately following a static hold appears sudden and disturbing. This effect is sometimes used deliberately (a whip-pan) for special effect, but normally movements begin (and end) gradually – i.e. the movement is *smoothed* in. This smoothing can be likened to smoothing curves in boats or aircraft, to assist water- or air-flow, and this is sometimes known as fairing. If a moving shot is required to begin with the subject stationary the calculation must include speeding up from the static position. The speeding up can be long or short as required. Fairing has to be done for each movement (E/W; N/S; rotation; zoom.)

Calculating fairings

The length of the speed-up is measured in time i.e. the number of frames it takes to reach the desired constant speed. For example A constant speed of 2.5 units can be achieved in four frames: $\frac{1}{2}$, 1, $1\frac{1}{2}$, 2 (the fifth frame would be $2\frac{1}{2}$ – and the first of the constant run). By adding a speed up at the start, however, the pan has been extended two frames. The distance used to reach the speed of 2.5 is 5 units (which would normally take only two frames but here takes 4). Naturally, the longer the speed-up, the more extra frames are needed. If extending the shot by 2 frames is acceptable then there is no problem. However, more often than not the number of frames is rigidly fixed. You may be able to use a slightly higher continuous speed, or manipulate the field sizes to lengthen or contract the distance between the two centres. A pocket calculator can be of great assistance.

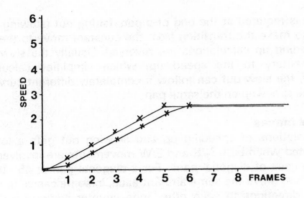

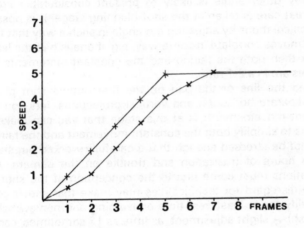

FAIRING IN MOVES

Speed up in 5 frames

Fairing in to constant speed of $2\frac{1}{2}$ increments in a total of 5 units (equivalent to 2 frames at constant speed) 1, 2, 3, 4–5 constant (10 units = 2 frames constant). This could be smoothed out $\frac{1}{2}$, 1, 2, 3, 4, $4\frac{1}{2}$–5 constants (15 units = 3 frames constant).

5 frame speed up to a constant of 5 increments

Similar fairings can be introduced in faster speed changes.

A few other examples

2, 4, 6, 8–10 constant (total of 20 = 2 frames at constant)

1, 2, 4, 6, 8, 9–10 constant (total of 30 = 3 frames at constant)

$2\frac{1}{2}$, 5, $7\frac{1}{2}$, 10, $12\frac{1}{2}$–15 constant (total 22 = $1\frac{1}{2}$ frames at constant)

If the same slow out is used then total number of frames 'lost' on fairing is 3.

1, 2, 3, 4, 5, 6, 7, 8, 9, 10, 11, 12, 13, 14–15 constant (total 105 = 7 frames at constant).

Speeding up and slowing out are much easier if the components are in simple ratios to each other.

Further Fairings

If a hold is required at the end of a pan, fairing out (slowing out) is needed to make the transition from the constant move to the static. The speeding up calculations are reversed. Usually the slow out is complementary to the speed up, which simplifies calculations. However, the slow out can follow a completely different curve from that of the speed up on the same pan.

Diagonal moves

The calculations of speeding up and slowing out gets a lot more complicated when both N/S and E/W movements are involved, such as in the case of diagonal pans. For a diagonal pan at 45° the two wheels must move the same amount each, in some cases, though, in opposite directions to each other (one counter adding up and the other subtracting). But at least the speeding up curves are identical. A pan at any other angle is likely to present considerable problems unless great care is taken at the shot-planning stage. It is possible to simplify calculations by adjusting the angle in such a way that the N/S and E/W moves corrolate in some way, e.g. if one is half the length of the other then both the fairing and the constant increments for the two moves are in a 2:1 ratio.

Drawing the line of the pan on the first outline shot plan, and making separate horizontal and vertical projections, lets you see its component movements. It is at this stage that you can make slight alterations to simplify both the constant movement and the fairings.

It cannot be stressed enough that a carefully worked out shot plan can save hours of frustration and trouble on the camera. Artistic considerations must come first in the conception of the shot, but a complete disregard for technicalities may make that shot a physical impossibility (or at least very time consuming and nervewracking to accomplish). A slight adjustment, as little as $\frac{1}{2}$° sometimes, can mean the difference between a well executed shot and a disaster.

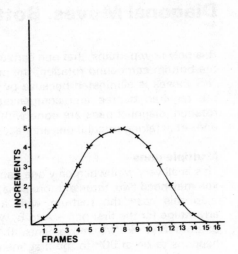

Continuous fairings
The fairing can last the full length
of the shot, either speeding up or
slowing down continuously; or
the slow out can start as soon as
the speed up has finished as here.

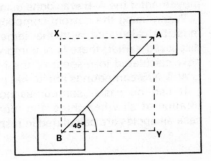

45° pans
A diagonal pan at 45° needs the
same E/W and N/S movements
(AX and BY) the constant
increment and fairings will also be
the same for both.

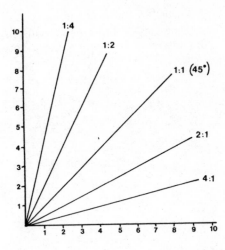

Other diagonal pans
A workable ratio between the
E/W and N/S movements should
be a major consideration when
diagonal pans are planned.

63

Diagonal Moves, Bottom Rotation

It is only now perhaps, that one can fully appreciate the usefulness of the bottom compound rotation; the problem of matching the E/W & N/S moves is eliminated because by setting the bottom rotation to the required degree and compensating for it on the top (table) rotation, diagonal pans are done with only one move; therefore only one set of fairing calculations are necessary.

Multiple pans

This is all very well when only one pan is involved during the shot but you may need two, three or more pans.

In this case the rostrum with a compound rotation has the advantage for the first pan – A to B, while B to C will require the use of both E/W & N/S movements. If the second line of pan (B-C) happens to be at 90° to the first line of pan (A-B) the problem does not arise because this move can be executed using the N/S movement if the A-B was done using E/W, or vice versa.

When using the bottom compound rotation the second movement must be calculated with the same considerations for the angles as discussed earlier; there is one important difference: all the angles are now calculated in respect of the first line of pan (A-B) because the E/W & N/S compounds are in that position now.

It can be easier sometimes not to use the bottom compound rotation at all when three and more positions are required in which case all angles are calculated in respect to the horizontal.

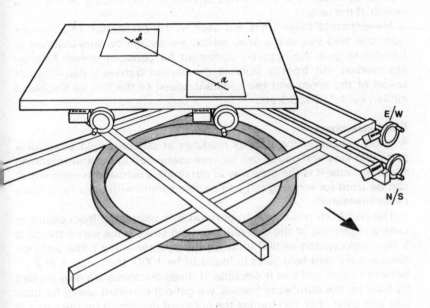

BOTTOM COMPOUND ROTATION

The rotation can be set at the correct angle so that the diagonal pan (from a to b) can be made by using the N/S movement only. The rostrum table is rotated on the top rotation to remain parallel to the horizontal of the camera.

T.A.S. F

Field Size Changes

If a change of field size is required during a pan, then the tracking movement of the camera has to be calculated in the same way as the pan; this obviously includes the fairing (speed up and slow out). This is done in much the same way as the calculations of the E/W & N/S movements, except that the units on the counter do not represent any specific units of measure such as inches or degrees as in the case of the other table movements. (1000 units on the counter can represent a distance equal to one field size or several – depending on the focal length of the lens.)

Nevertheless these units are used in the calculation of *distances* from one field size to the other which are divided by *time* (number of frames) to give the required increment for constant speed. Fairings are worked out from a suitable corrolation between the constant speed of the zoom and the constant speed of the pan as discussed earlier, i.e. 1:1; 2:1; 3:1 etc.

Field size chart

A chart indicating the various readings at different field sizes for a particular lens and gauge can be very useful during the shot-planning stage because it is the only way of obtaining a distance in units which can be used for working out compatible zooms with pans (which are easily measured).

The pan from position A to position B is calculated from centre to centre regardless of the difference in field sizes. If the pan distance is 5 in. – represented as 500 units on the counter – and if the distance between the two field sizes is found to be 1000, then a rotio of 2 : 1 between zoom and pan is possible. If these distances are now divided by time i.e. the number of frames, we get our constant speed for both pan and zoom. For 100 frames the constant increment for the pan will be 0.05 in. (5 units on the counter) and the zoom increment is then 10 units. The speed up (and slow out) for both moves also has to correlate, otherwise they will not reach their respective B positions simultaneously. A four frame speed up produces two extra frames which have to be accommodated and the two speed up curves are corrolated in the same 2 : 1 ratio as the 'constant' moves.

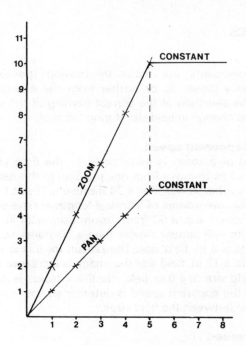

CHANGING FIELD SIZE

Speed up curve
In this case, the zoom and pan are correlated at 2 : 1 ratio.
ZOOM: 2, 3, 6, 8–10 constant (total 20 = 2 frames at constant SP).
PAN: 1, 2, 3, 4–5 constant (total 10 = 2 frames at constant SP).

Zoom and pans in practice
A sudden change in size and position can be used for a dramatic effect without
fairings.

67

Zooms

Zoom movements are made by moving (tracking) the camera progressively closer to or further from the artwork. Thus a zoom enables the selection of the correct framing of the shot, as well as a continuous change in field size during the shot.

Real and apparent speed

The speed of a zoom is determined by the time i.e. the number of frames it takes to move from one position to the next. So a 48 frame zoom (2 secs.) is slower than a 24 frame one (1 sec.) – in time at least.

However, two zooms of identical length in time can be different in apparent speed, e.g. a 50 frame zoom from a 24 in. field size to a 12 in. field size will appear slower than a 50 frame zoom from a 24 in. field size to a 6 in. field size. The reason for this is that from a 24 in. field size to a 12 in. field size the image is increased by 2 : 1 and from a 24 in. field size to a 6 in. field size this increase is in the ratio of 4 : 1. Therefore the apparent speed is determined not only by time but also by the ratio between the field sizes.

Relative speed

The relationship between the real speed at which the camera travels along the column and the apparent (visual) speed of the zoom depends on the location of that zoom on the logarithmic curve. A zoom from a 24 in. f.s. to a 12 in. f.s. will appear slower than a zoom using a physically shorter camera travel e.g. 12 in. f.s. to 4 in. f.s. in exactly the same number of frames – 100. The constant increments used for the first zoom will be larger (to cover a longer distance of track in the same amount of time i.e. frames) than those used for the second, although the apparent speed (visually) is slower. (In the first instance the size of the image is increased in the ratio of 2:1 and in the second the ratio increase is 3:1.)

ZOOM CALCULATION
CONSIDERATIONS

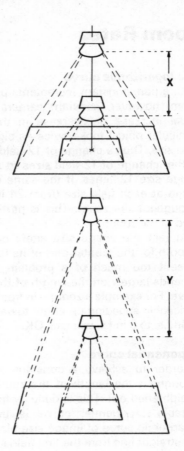

Zoom lens scale length
A lens of shorter focal length
(wide angle) has to travel a
smaller distance (X) to cover
identical field sizes as a lens of
longer focal length (Y).

Effect of field sizes
Two zooms, identical in length in
'time' (no. of frames) can have a
different apparent speed. Zoom
A-B will appear slower than zoom
A-C. (In fact the 'apparent' speed
of A-C zoom will be double that of
A-B).
If executed in the same number of
frames zoom D-E will appear
faster than zoom A-B, although
the camera in fact travels a longer
distance during the A-B zoom.

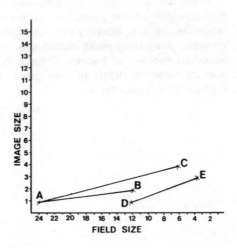

Zoom Rates

The logarithmic curve

With a pan, constant increments produce a constant change. With a zoom, however, constant camera movements do not produce an equal increase or decrease in the image size. For example, any particular object looks twice as big at a 12 in field size as at a 24 in field size. Thus a change of 12 field sizes doubles its size. However, a further change of 12 field sizes to a 1 in field size now increases the image size 12 times. If the same object is photographed using one frame at each field size (from 24 in to 1 in) it appears to accelerate throughout the zoom. This is particularly noticeable during the last third of the zoom.

In fact the image size alters on a logarithmic curve. It is quite smooth for the greater part of its length and therefore does not often present too much of a problem. Whether or not it is noticeable depends largely on the length of the zoom, and its location along the curve. For example a zoom – in from 24 in f.s. to 3 in f.s. will produce a noticeable speeding up effect towards the end, whereas a zoom from 12 in f.s. to 6 in f.s. will look OK.

Exponential curve

In order to achieve a constant, equal increase in the image size throughout the length of the zoom, the logarithmic curve must be straightened out. This is done by following an exponential curve. The suitable exponential curve is determined by reference to the logarithmic curve of image size plotted against field size. It is simply the straight line from the first field size to the last.

There are no constant increments during an exponential zoom, the entire length of the move has to be calculated. The normal fairing (speeding up and slowing out) has to be incorporated into the move as well, everything must match the table movements and fit into a specified number of frames. Clearly this is not the sort of operation that cameramen resort to very often, and the calculations are best made with a computer.

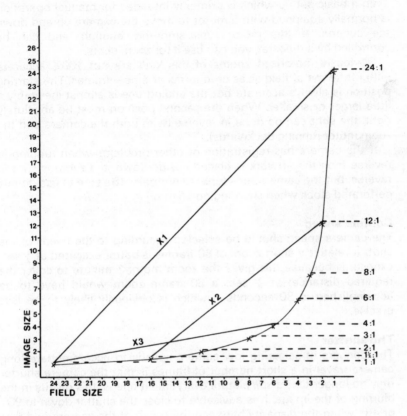

FIELD SIZE

EXPONENTIAL CURVES

As the camera is moved in (zoomed in) from the widest to the smallest field size in
equal increments, the object being photographed appears to increase in size. This
increase is not equal all the way along the track because the camera lens is
responding to a logarithmic curve. When the camera track follows an exponential
curve the increase in the image size is constant, e.g. X1 – 24 FS to 1 FS

                                        X2 – 16 FS to 2 FS
                                        X3 – 24 FS to 6 FS

71

Semi-Automated Zoom Operation

Even a basic set up which is primarily intended for manual operation is normally equipped with a motor to move the camera up and down the column. If this motor runs smoothly enough, and can be controlled by a rheostat, you can use it for zoom shots.

Obviously motorised zooms of this kind are not 100% accurate either in terms of field sizes or in terms of time – frames. The starting position is always accurate but the ending one is almost inevitably a little larger or smaller. When the second position must be absolutely right, the shot can be done in reverse (with both the camera and the zoom motor running backwards).

If the camera has registration or other problems when running in reverse then the artwork is placed upside-down, the zoom is shot in reverse, but the camera runs forward normally. (Be sure to use double perforated stock when shooting on 16 mm.)

Camera speed

The camera speed should be selected according to the needs of the shot. A relatively short zoom of 60 frames is better executed at $\frac{1}{2}$ sec. exposures because this gives the zoom motor 1 minute to cover the required distance; at $\frac{1}{4}$ sec. a 60 frame zoom would have to be accomplished in 30 seconds – which is obviously likely to be less precise.

The shutter

The dangers of selecting low camera speeds to accommodate long camera travel in a short number of frames is that the camera shutter may no longer take a *still* picture everytime it opens; this results in the blurring of the image. It is advisable to close the shutter down to 90° or 45° when the disparity between the speed of the camera and that of the zoom is too great. The blurring of the image is sometimes preferable to clear sharp images. For example, in the case of whip pans (very fast pans) the shot looks more realistic and strobing is eliminated (see p. 124).

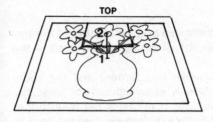
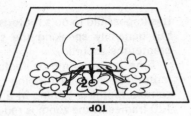

TOP

dOT

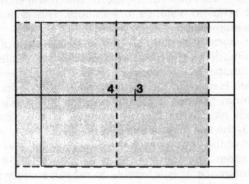

LENS APERTURE	F4	F5.6	F8	F11	F16
SHUTTER	11°	22½°	45°	90°	180°
EXPOSURE TIME	4 sec	2 sec	1 sec	½ sec	¼ sec

MECHANICAL ZOOM OPERATION

Shooting backward

To ensure greater accuracy at the final position (B) the artwork is placed on the rostrum table upside-down and the shot is executed as a zoom-out from B to A, the camera runs *forward* as normal. When the film is turned around for projection the shot is a *zoom-in* from A to B.

Calculating the lens centre

New corrected centre for shooting upside-down on 35mm; normal line up as done at academy aperture (3) then the E/W compound is moved to the new centre (4).

Shutter angle

If the shutter setting is altered exposure should be compensated with either the f stop or camera speed.

73

Calculating a Motorised Zoom

It is impossible to do a motorised zoom in a precise number of frames, but generally speaking the slower the shooting speed used – the greater the accuracy.

Time is the common factor between the camera and the zoom motor. For example, running continuously at an exposure of $\frac{1}{4}$ sec. the camera motor is turning at a rate of 120 revolutions per minute – or 120 frames. If the zoom is required to take 60 frames, then we have to find the appropriate speed of the motor which will enable the camera to travel the required distance in $\frac{1}{2}$ minute. This is done by trial and error using a stop-watch.

Once the correct setting on the rheostat control is found, an allowance is made for the speed up and slow out. While the camera is running continuously the rheostat control is brought into operation gradually until it reaches the predetermined setting for constant run. When the zoom reaches a certain position the slowing out begins. The slow out has to be just as smooth as the slow in. A sharp adjustment in the last minute will ruin the shot.

At the end of the shot – check the final position, and the number of frames the zoom has actually taken to ensure that it is within the acceptable tolerance. It is advisable to rehearse every shot against a stopwatch before it is actually taken.

Rheostat calibration

The rheostat controlling the speed of the zoom motor is normally calibrated in units of 1 – 100; a chart can be made up indicating the time it takes the camera to travel 1000 units on the counter at the chosen points on the rheostat (say 10, 20, 30 etc.) – this is indicated in seconds opposite each division of the rheostat scale.

It can give readings for every point on the rheostat control but even so, it can only be an approximation. The lengths of camera travel rarely fall into nice, easily divisible units, so an element of trial and error is still necessary in most cases. A scale alongside the rheostat control is easier to refer to although it may not be as detailed as a chart.

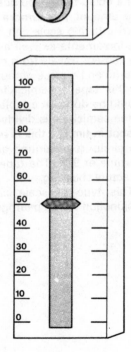

Calibrating the motor control
A scale for calculating the speed
of the zoom is made up and taped
to the outside of the rheostat
control pot. The timings are for
1000 units of track travel.

Digital controls
A digital control pot allows for
very detailed charts to be made
up for various distances.

Master control
This sliding rheostat control
overrides the speed control so
that all the functions can be
speeded up through the full scale
smoothly without changing
individual settings.

75

Independent Fairing for the Zoom

Whereas in the case of the diagonal pans the correlation between N/S and E/W movements has to be absolute if a straight pan line is to be followed, this is not quite the case with the zoom. If the speed up or slow out on the zoom takes a few frames longer it will not necessarily be unacceptable, as long as the two moves start and end together. The total number of frames at constant speed on the zoom naturally has to be shortened by the number of frames the speed up is extended.

In practice a close correlation between the zoom and the table moves is preferred because of both the ease of calculation and execution.

A shot plan may call for a constant pan from A to be in 100 frames while the zoom moves very gradually during the first 50 frames and then accelerates to arrive at pos. B at the same time as the pan. This type of zoom is calculated in two stages using two different constant speeds; the first (slower constant speed) to be faired (speeded up) into the second one.

Fairing scales

If the equipment used does not have a means of measuring the zoom (the amount the camera travels from one field size position to the next) a fairing scale can be prepared to give the speed up and slow out increments as well as the constant travel. The physical distance the camera travels from one position to the next is marked off on the column and a piece of tape is cut to that length. From the centre point on this tape a semicircle is drawn connecting the two ends (this should be done on a table or a large surface area). The circumference of the semicircle is divided by the number of frames required (length of shot in time) — this is best done in terms of degrees. Each point on the circle (representing one frame of the move) is "projected" onto the tape at 90°. The tape is then placed alongside the camera track for actual shooting.

This type of scale can also be used for panning moves in conjunction with a pantograph table.

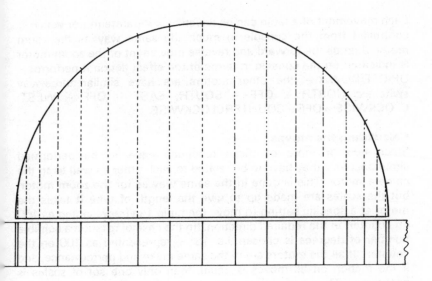

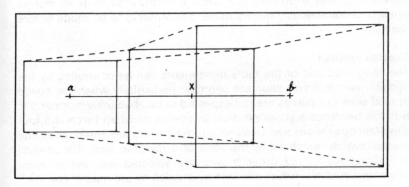

FAIRINGS AGAIN

Producing a fairing scale
A scale can be derived when the circumference of the half-circle is divided by the number of frames (length of the shot in time), and each point projected onto its diameter.

Fairings for pans and zooms
Pan from a to b is at constant speed while the zoom moves slower at first (A–X) and then accelerates (X–B).

Motorised Table Movements

Each movement of a table can be driven by a separate motor which is controlled from the console in much the same way as the zoom motor. Just as the forward and reverse movement of the zoom motor is indicated on the console in terms of the effect action it performs – UP/OFF/DOWN – the other motors are have similar three-way switches: NORTH – OFF – SOUTH; EAST – OFF – WEST; CLOCKWISE – OFF – COUNTERCLOCKWISE.

Calculating the moves

Since two or more of these functions have to be performed simultaneously they have to be related to each other as well as to the camera motor. This is done in the same way as for the zoom motor, but the scales are made up to give the length of time it takes the motor at a specific setting to move the table 1 in (represented as 100 on counter) in the required direction. (In the case of rotation a suitable number of degrees is chosen, i.e. 10° – represented as 100 on the counter). If all the motors are of the same make and performance, and if the friction on all moves is equal, then only one set of scales is necessary. The appropriate speed for each move is selected individually, and a dummy run (with a stopwatch) with all moves running simultaneously allows minor adjustments to be made before the take.

Master control

The zoom and one of the table movements can be controlled by the cameraman from two separate controls; particularly when the speed up and slow out curves are not expected to be absolutely compatible. But this becomes a sheer physical impossibility when three and four simultaneous moves are involved. So the motors are wired up to one master switch which takes the form of a rheostat also. The speeds and directions on all other moves are selected and set on their respective controls, which are then overridden by the master control.

A separate switch can be installed to disconnect each movement control from the master; this allows for the independent operation of one movement while the others still operate simultaneously.

☐☐☐ ◯	NORTH ↑ ⟋OFF ↓ SOUTH	**N/S**
☐☐☐ ◯	OFF WEST ⟋ EAST	**E/W**
☐☐☐ ◯	CLOCKWISE ⟋OFF ANTI-CLOCKWISE	**ROT**
☐☐☐ ◯	UP ⟋OFF DOWN	**ZOOM**

Rheostat scale: 100, 90, 80, 70, 60, 50, 40, 30, 20, 10, 0

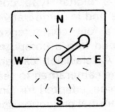

CONTROL OF MOTORISED MOVEMENTS

Control box

Each movement has its own rheostat and switch. The master control brings all the movements into operation simultaneously, speeding up and slowing down as necessary. Charts are made to give the time it takes to move a specific distance at various settings for each movement separately.

Joystick control

N/S and E/W movements can be operated simultaneously.

Fully Automated Operation

The motorisation of the camera movements speeds up the shooting process and is particularly useful for television work (stills for inclusion in documentary programmes). However, the tolerance required in both framing and lengths of shots make this type of operation unsuitable for most precision work demanding absolute accuracy (title sequences, commercials, special effects). By linking all movements and the camera motor to a digital-type computer, fully automatic shooting becomes possible with absolute precision.

The computer is programmed with the number of frames which moves should take, the initial and the final positions, the fairings (in percentages) and so forth. When all the variables are set, the whole is put in operation by a master switch. If necesssary, the operation can be stopped at any point. So holding, or bringing in another factor such as a dissolve, is simple. Another feature of this system is that it can repeat a move to a very high degree of accuracy which simplifies shooting with travelling mattes (see p. 138).

The advantages of fully automated shooting are enormous in terms of both speed and accuracy. A whole range of things which were previously considered too time-consuming and consequently expensive, becomes possible. A scene involving a great number of cel changes, which would normally be shot at a static field size, can now have a gentle movement added to it to emphasise a point or inject some life into an otherwise boring scene where only the lips of one or two characters move.

The last word in automation

Automation based on a digital type computer system gives a satisfactory performance and is comparatively inexpensive. However it is possible to obtain a fully computerised system where all the information is programmed into a computer which then carries out the operation required. A television camera attached to the reflex viewing system allows the cameraman to see the action on a monitor. A $\frac{1}{2}$ in or 1 in VTR machine, adapted for single frame recording, can then play back a take at normal projection speed immediately.

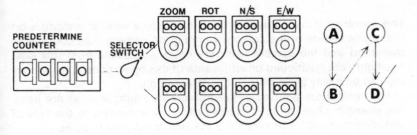

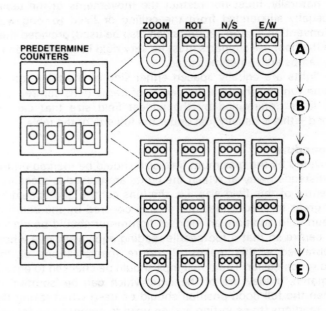

FULLY AUTOMATED ROSTRUM CONTROLS

Small control box
'A' represents the information at the start of the move and row 'B' the end of that move. A switch reverses the functions of these two rows so that a second move can then be accomplished from B to A. This way, by using only two sets of controls an endless number of moves can be made.
Note: the above controls are in addition to the normal camera controls.

Large control unit
When more than one row of controls are used it becomes possible to shoot an entire series of moves (including holds and dissolves) all in one go without stopping to re-set the controls. Each row has the complete information for the specific move which it governs so that different speed ups and slow outs can be used for different moves as well as different settings for the Exponential Zoom.

81

Lighting

The operational mechanism of the camera (on a vertical system) is on the opposite side of the column carrying the camera – all controls on the stand and the camera itself are easily accessible from this side. The lights are positioned on either side of this operational area so they too can be easily accessible to the cameraman.

For normal top lighting of flat artwork two light sources are used; the strength of these light sources can vary according to the type of shooting that will be required and the size of the area to be lit.

Top lighting
The lights, naturally, must not restrict the movements of the table. They are usually suspended from the ceiling or fixed to long wall brackets. Conventional lamp supports can also be used, provided they are fixed to the floor. All supports must be very rigid in construction as quite heavy lamps are sometimes used.

The two lights are equally spaced either side of the table, on an imaginary line running through the centre of frame (lens centre). The area to be lit is determined by the widest field size that can be photographed – this is usually just under the full size of the table.

Line up procedure
The area covered by the maximum field size should be marked on the table. The distance away at which the lights are placed is measured from the centre of this field size, i.e. the lens centre, and should be sufficiently great to ensure that this area is covered by the beam of the light source. In addition, an incident lightmeter should be placed at the lens centre so that a footcandle reading equivalent to a whole f stop is obtained – this makes all future manipulations of the exposure so much easier. The two lamps should be checked to ensure that they match, if they are of the type which can be 'spotted' or 'flooded' then the full flood position should be used when taking the foot candle readings (the spotting is then used to compensate for any loss of luminosity during the lifespan of the bulb; it can also be used to boost the lighting when the exposure requires it).

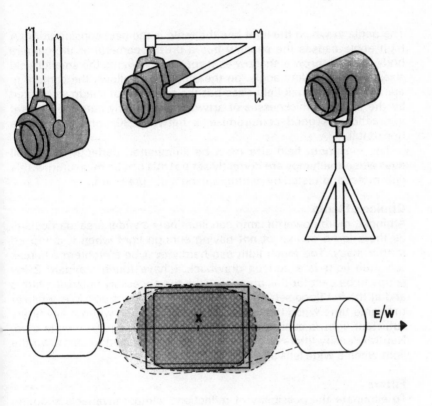

E/W

LIGHTING SUSPENSION SYSTEMS

Various ways in which the lights are mounted.

Even lighting
When measured separately at the table centre (X) each light gives the same
footcandle reading.

83

Lighting Considerations

The angle at which the light hits the table is the next consideration. A high angle causes the shadow board on the camera, or the camera body itself to throw a shadow as it zooms in towards the smaller field sizes. A very shallow angle, on the other hand, allows the camera to approach quite small field sizes but the problems of shadows created by the different thicknesses of artwork (particularly cutouts) make it impractical. A good compromise is between 30° and 35° to the horizontal.

The maximum field size must be illuminated perfectly evenly all over when the lamps are correctly set up, this can be measured with a lightmeter and tested by photographing a flat grey card.

Choice of lamp
A bigger, more powerful lamp can illuminate a wider area, particularly as there is no danger of not having enough light when it is moved farther away. Too much light can hardly ever be a problem whereas too little light is a serious drawback. I have found standard 2 kw lamps to be best for this purpose. With the necessary polarizing filters and at the full flood setting a good working f stop is possible, while at the same time when the lights are on full spot and without any filters sufficient light is available for interpositive printing off a white card. Neutral density filters or diffusion filters can be used to cut down the light when a wide lens aperture is required.

Filters
To eliminate the possibility of reflections, almost invariably shooting with top lighting is done through polarizing filters (both on the lights and the lens – see p. 98). These are usually suspended some distance in front of the lights. It is important that they do not get too hot, as this may destroy their polarizing properties. It is well worth the trouble of making a set of good filter mounts for the lights. You can then use any suitable filters with ease.

The barn-door fitting on the 2 kw lamp can be useful support for a filter mount which slides in from above. The mount is made of wood which is drilled to allow the loss of heat; the end nearest to the light is lined with a layer of asbestos. Several grooves at the wider end can accommodate a number of filters; these are mounted on square plywood frames which slide into the holder.

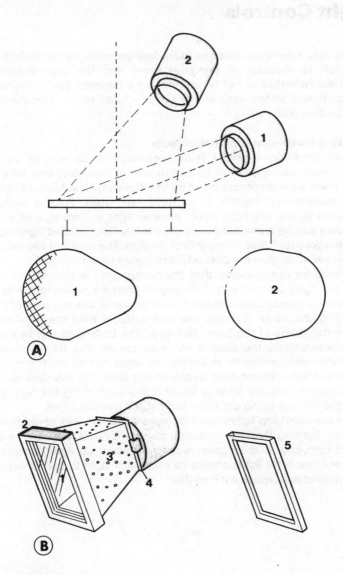

LIGHTING CONSIDERATIONS

A. Angle of lights

The small angles of incidence (1) produce rather uneven lighting over the full area of the table. Steeper angles produce more even spread, but it is still uneven and is compensated by the second light directly opposite and set at the same angle. The lamps are lined up to the centre of the table when this is itself lined up at the lens centre.

B. Lighting hoods

1, Filter holder for lights. 2, Filters are inserted from above. 3, Ventilation holes. 4, Asbestos backed rear end to prevent overheating. 5, Filter mount.

Light Controls

Lights may simply be wired to individual switches, or controlled by a 'dimmer' (a rheostat or thyristor) fitted into the control console. Switches (whether or not wired through a dimmer) can conveniently be positioned at the base of the stand – large robust switches may then be foot operated.

Lighting three-dimensional objects

A three-dimensional object lit by conventional top light as used for flat artwork, will appear to have two strong shadows; one on either side. Thus, such an object must be lit differently. The basis of lighting three-dimensional objects is to have one main shadow which is produced by the key light, while another light is used as a fill-in. The shadows can be eliminated with completely flat, diffused lighting, but this destroys the three-dimensional illusion. The angle of the key light can be varied to give the desired prominence to the shadow.

It must be remembered that the background is also lit mainly by this one light source, very low angles produce prominent elliptical shapes and greater unevenness in light between one extreme of the lit area and the other. So they are less suitable than the high angles where the shape of the beam falling on the table is nearer to a circle and consequently the area is more evenly lit. The fill light can be positioned independently at a different angle and its main function is to control the contrast ratio between the light and the dark sides of the object. A suitable level is found either by moving the light away from the table or using diffusion and neutral density filters.

The standard top lights used for normal flat artwork should not be used for lighting three-dimensional objects. Even if they can be positioned correctly, it is inconvenient to set them up again accurately. Two or more extra lights should be made available to the cameraman for any special purpose such as this.

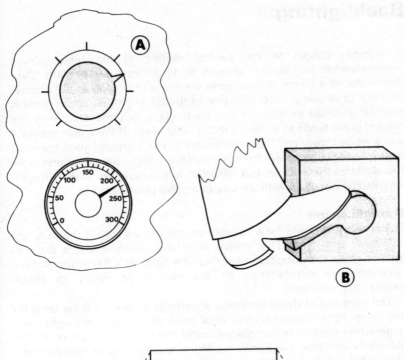

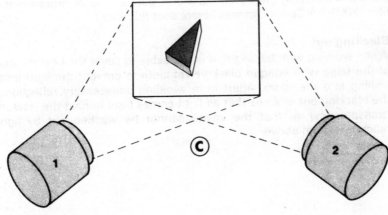

LIGHTING CONTROLS

A. Intensity control
Rheostat controlled light switch positioned on the console. This includes a voltage indicator.

B. On/off switches
Foot-operated switches make for ease of operation.

C. Lighting a three-dimensional object
1, Key light gives suitable modelling. 2, Fill light lightens shadows as needed.

87

Backlighting

A suitable cutout in the central section of the table allows transparencies and similar artwork to be lit from underneath. Over this is placed a piece of clear glass the same thickness as the groove. In order to obtain greater diffusion of the backlight, a ground glass is sometimes used in place of the clear glass, but the texture of the ground glass tends to show up in the clear areas of the transparency — e.g. a white cloud, etc. If it is necessary to use a ground glass then it is best placed farther away from the surface — focus area. Not only does this defocus the texture, but diffusion is increased as well. Diffusion can also be obtained with the use of a milky plastics sheet.

The light source
The primary requisite for a suitable source of backlight is that it is soft (diffused) and even. This means invariably using diffusers such as ground glass or bouncing (reflecting) the light off a flat white surface (sometimes a combination of the two is necessary to obtain satisfactory diffusion).

The simplest of these methods is perhaps to place a 2 kw lamp (or any other light source) on the floor level and bounce the light via a large white card or board placed under the table at an angle of 45°. (All shots involving the Earth, the Moon, Jupiter and its moons in the film "2001 – A Space Odyssey" were shot this way.)

Blacking out
When working with backlight, it is advisable to cover the bottom area of the table with opaque black velvet cloth to prevent the light from spilling into the room. Apart from avoiding unnecessary reflections, the blacking out ensures that all light comes from behind the artwork (transparency) so that the image cannot be washed out by light reaching it from above.

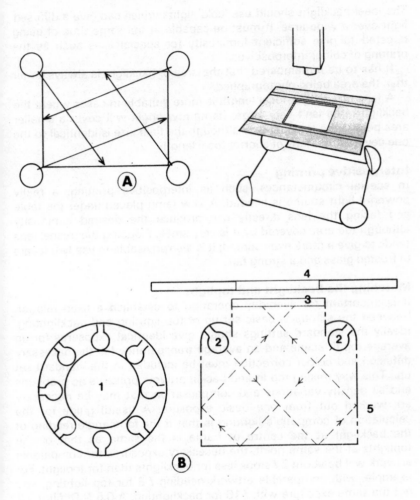

BACKLIGHTING

A. **Simple set-up**
Four quartz-iodine lamps bounced off a board with white formica top. The lights are lined up as above to give even illumination over the whole area.

B. **Diffusing drums**
1, Lights are put round the edge of the drum. Cross section shows how light from the bulbs (2) is reflected from white walls to the ground glass (3). 4, Clear glass in the table cutout. 5, Ventilation holes.

Ideal Backlight

The ideal backlight should use 'cold' lights which can give a diffused light over a wide area. It must be capable at the same time of being boosted to give sufficient luminosity for special uses such as the printing of colour interpositives.

It has to be remembered that the area of backlight is always larger than the area being photographed.

A lens of a longer focal length is more suitable in cases where the backlight area isn't very large; its narrow angle will cover a smaller area behind the transparency although the field size is identical to the one covered by a lens of shorter focal length.

Interpositive printing

In special circumstances, such as interpositive printing, a really powerful light source is needed. A 2kw lamp placed under the table and facing the lens directly can produce the desired luminosity although the area covered by it is very small. Flopping the fresnel lens tends to give a more even spread; it is also advisable to use two layers of frosted glass and a strong fan.

Matching the backlight and toplight

It is important for everyday operation to establish a fixed relation between the standard, basic set up of top lighting and backlighting. Ideally the standard settings should give identical exposures for an average top lit scene and an average transparency (all the necessary diffusion and colour correction must be included in the standard set up.) This way mixing top lit and backlit artwork presents no problems and all density variations and compensation that may be necessary are worked out from one basic exposure. A useful guide for the calculation of compatible lighting is that if the footcandle reading of the backlight at the centre of frame is the same as that of the toplights at the same point, the necessary exposures for comparable artwork will be about 2 f stops less for backlights than for toplight. For example, with comparable artwork needing f 8 for top lighting, you get the same exposure with f 16 for backlighting. A 0.6 N.D. filter − 2 stops − placed between the backlight source and the artwork will make the backlight exposure compatible with the toplight i.e. both f8.

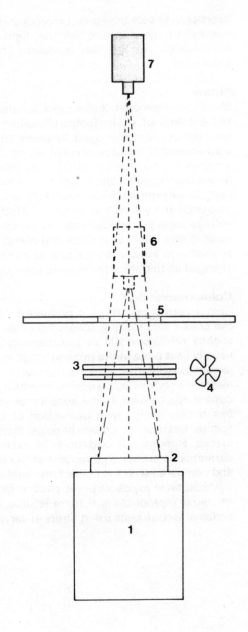

Using a 2KW lamp for printing
In order to obtain perfectly even illumination over the whole frame the position is determined by the angle of acceptance of the lens when the size of the light source is limited. A larger working area is obtained on the table top with a narrow angle lens.
1, 2K Lamp. 2, Fresnel lens flopped to give more even light. 3, Two layers of frosted glass (separated). 4, Cooling fan. 5, Table top cutout with clear glass. 6, Camera position when longer focal length lens is used. 7, Camera position when shorter focal length lens is used.

Colour Temperature

In order to ensure the correct reproduction of colour it is essential that the colour temperature of the light source should match the specifications of the film emulsion. This is usually represented in kelvins (K).

Filters

Most colour negative movie stock is balanced for 3200 K lighting. This is the colour of studio lamps (including tungsten halogen). A colour temperature meter is used to check the colour temperature of the light source. It indicates the degree of correction required – which is accomplished by the use of coloured filters. These are made of gelatin or acetate (colour compensating or colour printing filters). They are used in varying densities from 0.05 to 0.50 in primary colours (cyan, magenta, and yellow and sometimes red, green & blue). A variation in voltage supply produces changes in colour temperature of the light source; and it can also change towards the end of a bulb's life. It is advisable to keep a log (or just notes in a diary) when the bulbs are changed so that this can be done at regular intervals.

Colour correction

Colour correction makes it possible to produce subtle alterations to the colour balance of a scene. This may be needed, for example, if a slightly off-colour still or transparency is to be used. Correction is usually best done at the printing stage in the laboratory, but this is not always possible because two scenes may be linked together with a dissolve or other optical device. In which case the correction has to be done in the camera. In the absence of any other aids the cameraman has to rely on his own perception of colour balance; if one of the scenes has correct colour balance then the second one should be placed alongside it and both lit evenly. The scene which needs correction is examined through a series of colour compensating filters and compared with the correct one until a suitable filter is found.

Variation in exposure is yet another factor that affects the accuracy of colour reproduction. If there is time, the wisest course is to do a series of wedge tests using filters at varying exposures.

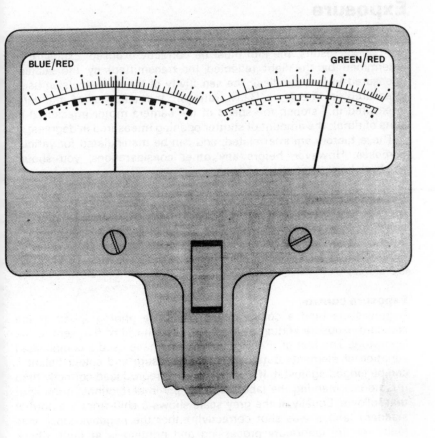

COLOUR TEMPERATURE

Colour meters

Colour temperature meters have a photocell and two filters (usually red and blue).
Some models use three filters – red, blue and green and are more accurate.

Relative proportions of red and blue (or red, blue and green) light are indicated on a
pre-calibrated scale and can be converted to kelvins or mireds. Some models give a
direct reading in kelvins as well as a recommended filter for a specific type of colour
emulsion.

C.C. filters

A typical range includes red, blue, green, yellow, cyan, and magenta filters in
varying densities.

Red	05R	10R	20R	30R	50R
Blue	05B	10B	20B	30B	50B
Green	05G	10G	20G	30G	50G
Yellow	05Y	10Y	20Y	30Y	50Y
Cyan	05C	10C	20C	30C	50C
Magenta	05M	10M	20M	30M	50M

The colour correction of other strengths are obtained by a combination of the above
e.g. 40R from 30R + 10R.

93

Exposure

For correct results, the film must be correctly exposed. Exposure is determined by the light reflected (or transmitted) by the subject (measured in foot-candles); the sensitivity of the film emulsion used (measured in A.S.A or D.I.N. ratings); the aperture of the lens (measured in *f* stops); the speed of the camera motor (measured in units of time); the amount of shutter opening (measured in degrees).

These factors are interrelated, and can be manipulated for various purposes. However, before any other considerations, you should establish basic exposure needed.

Exposure charts

An exposure chart contains the basic standard exposures for different types of film stock with standard toplighting and backlighting. In addition it carries the compensations needed for very close-up work right down to 1 : 1 filming. (The exposure compensation at this point is 2 stops.)

Exposure control

A grey scale (and a colour chart) should be photographed at the standard exposure setting at the head of each roll of film sent to the laboratory. The rest of the shot, which may have used a complicated variation of elements determining the exposure and colour balance, can be judged against it. If the grey scale is reproduced correctly then it is no use blaming the laboratory for any imperfections in the shot that follows. Equally, if the grey scale shows a shift from the normal standard (and it was shot correctly), either the negative stock was faulty, or the laboratory processing and printing is at fault. Check immediately with your laboratory, and arrange for them to find out what went wrong.

Information

A camera slate should carry as much useful information as possible. A great many combinations of elements could be involved and these are not always easy to recall if it is necessary to re-shoot. Also a shot requiring a similar solution may turn up several weeks later.

All laboratory reports and the cameraman's notes relating to the actual move and his comments on the result should all be filed for reference.

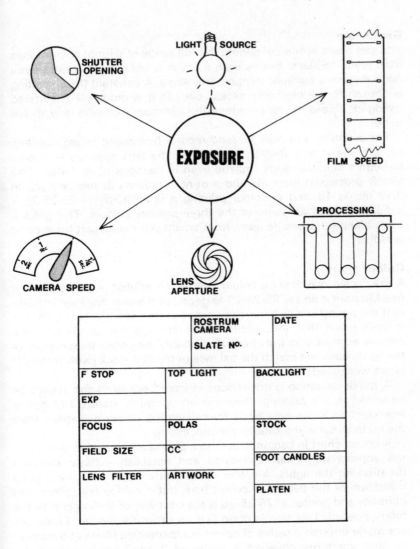

EXPOSURE

	ROSTRUM CAMERA SLATE NO.	DATE
F STOP	TOP LIGHT	BACKLIGHT
EXP		
FOCUS	POLAS	STOCK
FIELD SIZE	CC	FOOT CANDLES
LENS FILTER	ARTWORK	
		PLATEN

EXPOSURE

A number of factors control the final negative density. Light level, lens aperture, shutter opening, and camera speed control the light reaching the film. The effect of that light is determined by the film speed, and the processing.

Typical rostrum slate
Slates should give as much information as possible. This ensures that you can repeat the shot if necessary.

95

Exposure Aids

Grey scale

You can use a scene containing the full range of neutral colour tones from white to black. But as such a scene is not easy to come by you normally use a suitably stepped grey scale. A constant (fixed) setting is chosen for all elements except one. That is progressively altered (wedged) across the range where the optimum exposure is expected to be.

For example, you may fix *(and record)* film speed rating, lighting, camera speed and shutter angle. Then the lens aperture is altered through a suitable range (maybe even in fractions of an *f* stop.) The film is processed normally and a print is ordered at *middle light;* in B/W this is 13, and in colour printing it is *25 across* – 25-25-25 – indicating equal amounts of the three primary colours. This gives a basic standard exposure level, from which you can depart for specific reasons.

Colour chart

A grey scale may have a colour cast when printed at 25-25-25. The need to print it on say 28-24-23 to get rid of the cast does not indicate that the negative was incorrectly exposed (the average is still 25) but it does mean that the colour reproduction is not accurate. If the original artwork was truly neutral, probably the colour temperature of the lights does not match the balance of the film stock (with whatever filters were used).

A minor deviation is not serious in itself because it can always be corrected in the printing. However an optimum standard of colour reproduction is the only basis for calculating colour deviations from the norm either in the shooting or processing.

A colour chart in conjunction with a grey scale is used to determine the appropriate colour correction and establish a basic standard filtration for the lights. A colour temperature meter will give a good indication of the degree of colour bias, but a wedge test, processed normally and printed at 25-25-25 is the best way of finding exactly the filters needed. This test is done like an exposure wedge. Exposures are made through a series of colour compensating filters at a number of lens apertures covering a range of 1 or 2 stops around the calculated exposure. Colour compensating filters absorb the light proportionally to their strength (density), so a colour correction wedge has to be linked with exposure.

GREY SCALE

2%	4%	10%	18%	38%	60%	93%

COLOUR CHART

RED	GREEN	BLUE	YELLOW	CYAN	MAGENTA

EXPOSURE TEST CHARTS

Grey scale

This is a series of neutral colour patches of progressively greater density. It is useful for exposure determination.

Colour chart

For colour film, it is imperative to know the effect of exposure on the various colours. Suitable colour patches are available combined to form charts. These help to pin down stock defects, exposure errors, lighting, processing and so on as the cause of colour problems.

97

Filters

Polarizing screens

Polarizing screens are normally essential for top-lit shooting. They eliminate most reflections and suppress the effect of some dust particles. Screens are used on each light and on the camera lens. Plastic polarizing screens are suitable for the lights, but the one in front of the camera lens should be of *cine* quality glass, and free from any optical distortions.

Polarizing filters restrict light to one plane of polarization. The plane is usually indicated on the screen by an arrow. If you use filter holders, these too can be conspicuously marked. It is of prime importance that all the polarizing screens are lined up correctly in relationship to each other. Those on the lights (usually, of course just two) are used with their arrows pointing in the same direction. The polarization plane of the lens screen should be set at 90° to the polarization plane of the others. If the polarisation plane is not marked on the filters, their relative angles can be established by rotating one filter against any other. Most light gets through when the two planes are parallel, and hardly any light is visible at 90°.

The lens filter must be firmly mounted, because any rotation would change the light transmission, affecting the exposure.

Types of polarizing screen in use

For normal colour work it is important to choose a polarizer which has little or no effect on the colour temperature of the light. The effectiveness of a screen is related to its strength. Strong screens absorb a lot of light, and are not always truly neutral in colour. A good compromise is achieved by Polaroid type *H.N. 38*

A much stronger Polaroid type *H.N. 22* is extremely useful for titling superimpositions where colour balance is not critical.

White lettering on a shiny black paper (cartridge type) or on black glossy and glazed photographic paper, can be superimposed over a scene already shot, on the second run through the camera without any danger of 'washing out' the background when these Polaroids are used. In fact several runs through the camera are possible. Such a filter, however, is not suitable for normal shooting as it is difficult to colour correct adequately; it also increases the contrast ratio to a very high degree.

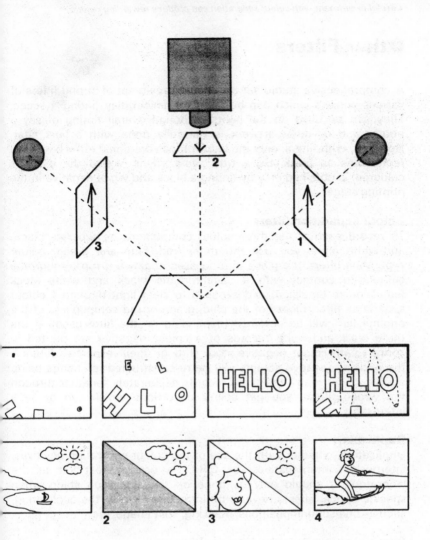

FILTERS

Polarizers
Polarizing filters in front of the lights are positioned so that their polarisation axes are parallel. The lens polarizer is positioned so that its polarisation axis is 90° to the axis of the other two filters.

Multiple shooting
You may want to shoot a number of differently moving elements, for example letters to make a title. This may need many passes through the camera (one for each letter) and very strong polarizers are needed if top-lit. The colour distortion is unimportant in the case of white super-impositions because they are 'burnt in' over the existing scene.

Masking off sections (split-screen)
With normal polarisation, a section of the screen can be masked off with a piece of shiny black paper so that on the second run another scene can be photographed in that area, with opposite masking.

99

Other Filters

A comprehensive studio set up should have a set of strong filters of various colours which can be used for deliberatley tinting a scene. They can be used on the lights, although overall tinting of say a photograph or other artwork is normally done with a lens filter. However, with filters, only the lighter tones are tinted – the black still reproduces as black. So a true *sepia* effect (where the black is coloured) is obtained only by tinting a black and white negative in the printing stage.

Colour separation filters

To record each of the three colour components as separate black-and-white films, you use the three (red, blue and green) colour separation filters. If a piece of processed negative is run through the camera in contact with a panchromatic black and white stock (emulsion to emulsion) and exposed to clear light through a colour separation filter, record of the blue, green or red components of the original film will be obtained (depending on the filter used). If the three black-and-white records of a colour negative are printed in contact with colour negative stock through their respective filters – the original negative colours will be re-constructed (all things being equal). If you marry the three records deliberately together through the wrong filters, you get colour distortions which can be very interesting.

Duplicating

Duplication, whether with the use of the colour separation positives, interpositive/internegatives, or C.R.I., is usually best left to the laboratory. It should only be done on the animation stand when specific optical effects have to be introduced during the duplicating, such as title superimpositions, masking, split image, etc.

Combining images with interpositives

A sunflower shape is cut out of black paper to give a male and female matte. The background scene is printed on clear light and, at a specified frame, the male matte – representing the shape of the sunflower is placed on the table, and the printing continues. During the second run, the sunflower piece of interpositive is loaded in the camera (in sync) and printed through the female matte. If the shutter is kept open for only ten frames and then closed for another ten frames, and this process is repeated several times, then a third inter-positive can be used for the third run in the camera and exposed through the same female matte as the sunflower, only in reverse phase; the final composite has a sunflower alternating with a girl in the same outline superimposed on the background.

100

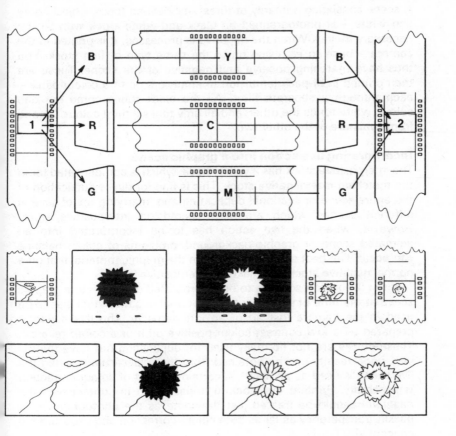

DUPLICATING PROCESSES

Colour separation
The original negative (1) is printed separately on to three pieces of panchromatic film through three colour separation filters (blue, green and red). This produces separate records of the yellow, magenta and cyan elements of the image. Printing through the same three separation filters on to colour negative stock produces a duplicate colour negative (2).

Combination printing
Suitable mattes on the rostrum table allow you to combine different film elements while printing in bipack.

Bipack Printing Effects

Tinting
A scene consisting primarily of three well defined tones – black, grey and white – is photographed on black-and-white stock with all the necessary moves. When the negative is processed, it is printed in the camera – base to emulsion on to the same type of film stock. You thus have matching positive and negative of the scene. These are then printed in bi-pack (emulsion to emulsion) on to a colour stock – each through a separate filter. All the black tones come out one colour, white tones the other; and all grey tones a third colour, formed from a mixture of the other two.

Incorporating live action into a graphic scene
The interpositive stock has a yellow base, which is compensated for in the matching internegative stock. This is fine for direct duplication of the entire scene or sectional duplicating and 'marrying up' of several different scenes which are all prepared on interpositive stock. However, when the live action has to be incorporated into an animated scene or graphic background, problems of colour balance can occur. The best solution is to shoot the graphic material first on a normal negative stock and make an interpositive from it.

If the live action scene is to be incorporated directly into a graphic scene at the time of shooting, then a normal negative stock has to be used in the camera instead of an internegative. The live action is prepared on a low contrast colour positive print or a colour reversal. These stocks are not normally used for duplicating but nevertheless very good results can be obtained from them, particularly when the live scene is used as an insert. A certain amount of colour correction is necessary. Printing the stock in bi-pack (and in contact with the negative) should be treated just the same as the photography of a backlit transparency as far as both colour correction and exposure are concerned.

Pre-fogging the negative stock in this instance helps to reduce the overall contrast. This is done by running the raw stock through the camera prior to the duplicating run; exposing to clear light. Obviously the extent of fogging has to be determined by an exposure wedge test.

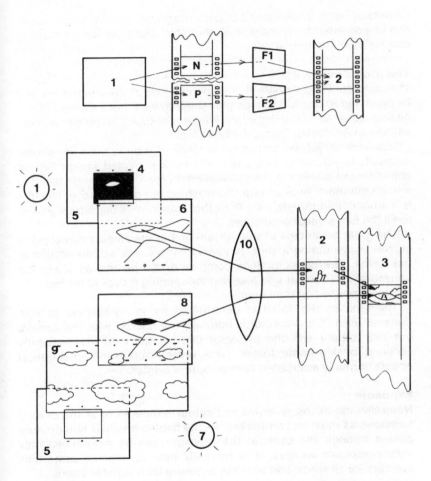

PRINTING EFFECTS

Tinting
Negative and positive black-and-white records are made from the original scene
(1). These are then printed through separate colour filters to tint both highlights and
shadows on a colour negative (2).

Combination
To include a live action pilot in an animated aeroplane. First, with backlight (1) the
pilot is printed from a positive (2) in bipack with negative stock (3). A mask (4) is
placed accurately on the table (5) with the aid of the plane cel (6). Then with top
light (7) the plane cel, with cockpit blacked out (8) is shot. The clouds (9) are moved
as needed. The camera and lens (10) remain fixed.

Back Projection

Instead of being loaded into a bi-pack magazine, the live action scene can be projected from underneath the table. The graphics are made in opaque paint on normal cels.

The projector

The projector is commonly located on one side of the stand base; and its beam is redirected towards the table top via a front silvered mirror positioned at 45°. The projected image is focused in the same plane as the camera focus. That is the table top.

If a back-projection screen, or a piece of ground glass (or similar material) is placed at this point, the back-projected image can be filmed by the camera in the conventional way. Care must be taken to darken the room in order to avoid washing out of the image. The film is rewound, and the graphics then shot (toplit) on a black background to fill the film's unexposed areas.

The great advantage of this system is that the camera can zoom in on the image during a shot, or simply 'blow-up' a certain section of the frame. The projector lens compound can be moved along the horizontal and vertical axis allowing for panning moves to be added to the zoom or used on their own.

The limit of the zoom is determined by the graininess of B.P. material used. The projector is normally interlocked with the camera but the camera and the projector can be operated independently allowing for skip-frame, freeze-frame, reverse action and other optical effects normally associated with an optical printer.

Exposure

Naturally, the exposure levels and colour temperature of the several components must be compatible. As the filming involves two or more passes through the camera, the exposure can be determined only with *composite wedges*. It is normally best to use the same lens aperture for all shots, and alter the exposure with suitable filters.

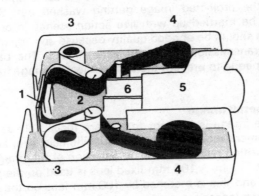

BACK PROJECTION

Suitable projectors are specially made for back projection on the animation stand.
The film passes through the gate (1) with a normal intermittent movement. This
may be synchronised to the camera shutter mechanism. It is driven by sprockets
(2). Two sets of chambers (3, 4) allow bipack projection. Light from the lamp (5) is
focused on the gate by a condenser system. Filters may be introduced in a slot (6)
between the lamp house and film gate. The projection lens is normally a separate
unit.

Aerial Image Projection

Aerial image back projection enables the simultaneous use of normal top-lighting. A pair of condensers are used. The top (flat) surface of the upper condenser is in the focus plane of the camera (i.e. in the backlight cutout on the table). The image from the projector is only visible through the camera lens or when a piece of grease-proof paper or similar semi-transparent material is placed on the condenser surface. The projector focus is set in this way.

The aerial image set up can be looked upon as a complex optical system enabling the camera lens to photograph the film in the projector gate. Top lighting can be used at the same time without any danger of the projected image getting washed out. So animated scenes can be married up with live action scenes in one pass. The artwork cels should be of good quality because any imperfections can affect the transmission of the projected image. The painted areas should be opaque to prevent the back-projected image from breaking through.

Using the aerial image

Because the image is brought to a sharp focus only at the camera gate, the camera must be used at a specific field size; any deviation from this position results in loss or distortion of the image. This field size is about $11\frac{1}{2}$ in. A 100 mm fixed lens is used on the projector for 35 mm film and this is matched by 100 mm lens on the camera. For 16 mm, 55 mm lenses are used.

Skip-framing, reverse action, and other optical effects can be accomplished easily with an aerial image projector while animated artwork or titles are being photographed at the same time. Panning along the back-projected image is also possible if the projector lens is fitted to a compound.

The condensers are mounted in the backlight cutout area of the rostrum table, which means that none of the table compound moves can be used. The artwork on the table-top has to be moved by some other means. The top and bottom peg-bars make E/W panning of the artwork possible but N/S and diagonal pans need the floating peg-bar.

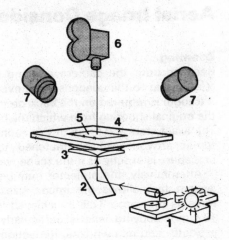

Table set-up
1, Projector. 2, Front-surfaced
mirror. 3, Condensers. 4,
Animation table. 5, Focus plane.
6, Camera. 7, Normal top lighting.

Condensers
A pair of plano-convex lenses
focus the projector image onto
the camera gate. The top surface
of the upper condenser lies in the
same plane as the artwork table.

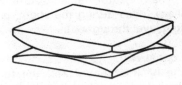

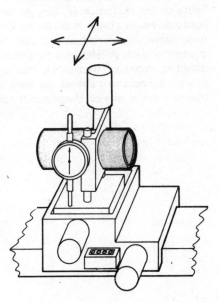

Projector lens
The projector lens may be
mounted in its own compound.
This gives precise adjustment to
the selection of back projection
frame area.

107

Aerial Image Considerations

Zooming

Because both the camera and the projector are locked in a rigid relationship to the condensers, conventional zooming is not possible. If a zoom is required on the back-projected image it should be done in the original shooting from which the back projection plate is prepared. The exact start and finish of this zoom can be determined so that the top-lit artwork can be matched to it; otherwise the marry up procedure is exactly as if the scene were static.

Alternatively, the projector may be fitted with an auxillary optical system that allows the image size to be altered while the focus remains the same. This is achieved with the use of an extra lens (a 152 mm copying lens is particularly suitable) placed between the projector and its own lens. Reduction and enlargement of the image in the projector gate results when the lens compound is moved towards and away from the projector; changing the field size projected on the condensers.

The projector has an auto-focus system which keeps the image in sharp focus during the zoom, and an auto-iris to ensure a constant light level throughout.

Exposure

The back-projected and the top-lit scenes are both photographed simultaneously by the same lens. Compatibility of exposure between the two scenes can be achieved with neutral density filters on the top lights or the projector. (Filters go between the projector gate and the light.) A visual check is possible; by looking through the camera the two elements of the scene can be seen as one composite. It is essential to establish basic exposures and colour correction for all the different types of film stock that are likely to be used both in the projector and the camera, as well as the basic top-light set-ups, so that any variations on these can be more easily calculated.

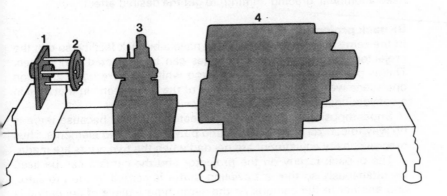

AERIAL IMAGE PROJECTOR

Projector set-up to give zooming facility
1, Fixed lens. 2, Field lens. 3, Copying lens and lens compound (the compound
moves along the base as well as enabling E/W and N/S movements of the lens). 4,
Projector (can also be moved along the base). This projector can also operate as a
one lens system when variation of the field size (zooming) is not required. The
image quality is then enhanced slightly.

109

Projection Considerations

Colour correction

The colour compatibility between the two or more scenes that go to make up one composite picture is just as important as their relative exposures. The exposure charts should show the standard colour correction filter pack normally used for a specific stock. The colour temperature of the light source (projector bulb) may require a basic correction and will alter if the voltage varies. Additional correction is added for each type of stock used. However each specific print may need additional 'grading' (timing) to get the desired effect.

Bi-pack projection

In the same way as the camera can have a bi-pack facility, so can the projector. Two superimposed images can be projected and printed. This is particularly useful where large white (or very light) areas on one scene would burn out the image of the other scene in that area in a conventional sequential double-exposure approach.

Superimposing images in the projector is limited because there is no way to control the exposure ratio between the two elements. Thus precise density adjustment are needed when the two prints are made.

The bi-pack facility on the projector and the camera can be used simultaneously so that a travelling matte is carried in the projector, and another in the camera. At the same time a piece of animation is being added to the back-projected scene. The other two components of the scene are added on separate runs through the camera with the use of their respective counter-mattes.

Registration

Registration of the projected image is just as important as that of the unexposed negative in the camera. The projector gate is normally equipped with negative registration pins and the scenes to be used for back-projection should normally be printed on negative perforated stock. The projector gates are mostly interchangeable and it is possible to use a film with positive perforations in a suitable gate.

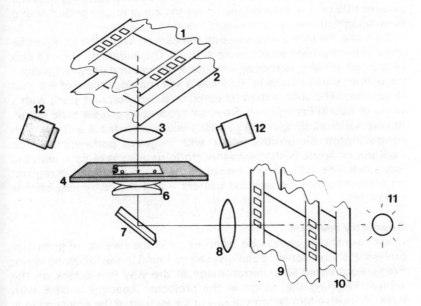

AERIAL IMAGE

Adding
By rotoscoping each frame of a live action sequence and tracing out key positions it
is possible to add an animated character dancing with a live action one.
Alternatively, a colour caption or an animated title can be 'superimposed' on a live
scene in one go.

All systems go
It is possible to use two separate travelling mattes, cel artwork, and a back
projection plate all in one go.
1, Raw stock. 2, Travelling matte in contact (bi-pack) with raw stock. 3, Camera
lens. 4, Table. 5, Cel artwork. 6, Condensers. 7, Front silvered mirror. 8, Projector
lens. 9, Back projection plate (B.G. scene). 10, Travelling matte in contact with BP
plate. 11, Projector lamp. 12, Top lights.

Uses of Back Projection

Intelligent use of the full rostrum camera facilities can save a lot of time in the preparation of animation artwork.

The effect of an animated character walking towards the camera can be achieved in two ways. Basically the background can appear to recede behind the man, or it can appear static while the man gets progressively larger. Both of these shots take a long time to animate fully and must be very precisely drawn to succeed.

Using back projection to make the background move, a perspective shot is photographed on its own — with the camera zooming out. The print of this take is then projected on the aerial image projector and married up with the cycle of cels of the man walking.

To make the man move towards the camera while the background stays still is perhaps a little more difficult. The animation cycle of cels of the man walking is shot against black background on reversal stock while the camera zooms in. This way a self-matting record of the shot is obtained. The shot is then repeated on a high contrast stock with a white or backlit background. Reversal processing gives a male matte. (If reversal processing is not available you must make a suitable high contrast print on positive stock with negative perforations.) The background scene is shot with this matte running in bi-pack with the raw stock. The self-matting record of the scene is printed in register on a separate run through the camera — and the composite shot is complete!

Geometry reversal
Great care should always be taken to avoid the reversal of geometry (unless it is intentional). Solutions can be found in the following ways: Preparing artwork in a mirror-image of the way it will look on the screen. Flopping the image in the projector. Loading bi-pack with base of positive film facing the raw stock instead of the emulsion may also be necessary in special cases.

Zooming background
The zoom out on the background artwork is done as a back projection plate which is then 'married up' on the aerial image with the cycle of cels of the man walking.

Zooming the foreground
The animation cycle is shot against black background as the camera zooms in. This gives a self-matting positive. The same shot is then repeated on Hi-con stock with back lighting to give the counter matte. The background scene can then be photographed through this counter-matte. The self-matting positive is then printed onto the same piece of film.

113

Other Projection Gadgets

Slide projector
Large format transparencies can be photographed directly but smaller format material must be projected. A slide projector can be used in the same way as a film projector from below the table. Alternatively the entire assembly may be housed in a box on top of the table, it can then be moved about like artwork.

Movie projection on the table top
A back-projection device like the one described above can be made using a small 16mm film projector so that a 'live' scene can be moved around the screen area as required. Our example of an animated plane and live action pilot (see p. 102) can now be done in such a way that the plane (carrying the projected image of the pilot) travels across the screen from one end to the other as well as moving closer or farther away from the camera.

Front projection
Front-projection material reflects the light back to its source directly along the same axis. It can be used as the background on the artwork table. A slide projector (or small 16mm film projector) is used to project the background image directly along the lens axis via a semi-silvered mirror set at 45°. The material reflects several hundred times more than the artwork on the cel placed over it. When the artwork is lit in the normal way this kills the projected image entirely. So it only comes out on the film in the clear areas of the cel. The painted areas record normally.

This system allows great manoeuvrability of the artwork, because the table movements are restricted only by the size of the front projection material and the artwork — but the projected image is static. Zooming is only possible if the fixed focal length lens on the camera is replaced by a zoom lens. If the artwork is moved on the N/S or E/W compound during the zoom (in order to zoom into an area from the centre) a drift will result between the front-projected image and the top-lit artwork; the zoom on the front-projected image will always be at the lens centre and is unaffected by the table movements (as long as the projection area is covered by the screen). This discrepancy can be exploited deliberately to give some interesting effects.

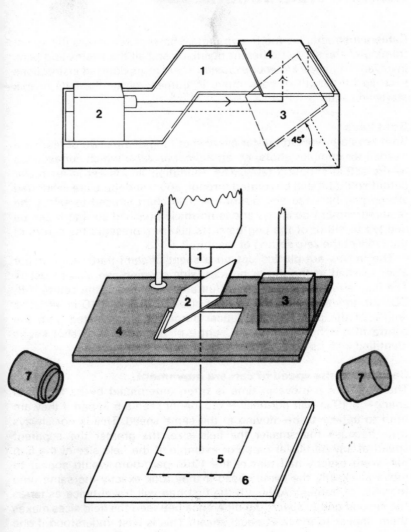

OTHER PROJECTION GADGETS

Table top projection unit

A simple unit to take still or movie projectors.
1, Black wooden box. 2, Projector (slide or specially adapted 16mm). 3, Front silvered mirror. 4, Back projection screen.

Front projection unit

Front projection images are projected along the lens axis, then back to the camera from highly reflective materials.
1, Camera lens. 2, Two-way mirror. 3, Projector. 4, Shadow Board. 5, Front projection material. 6, Rostrum table. 7, Top lights (polarised).

Camera Instructions

Camera instructiuons are in two parts. The *shot key* shows the actual framing of the shot at different positions and all the zooms and pans involved. The *dope sheet* or *exposure sheet* gives detailed instructions such as the length of each move in frames, where the fade or mix starts and ends.

Shot keys

Shot keys are worked out for every shot (sometimes two or more are needed for complex shots) on an *animation table* which corresponds to the actual shooting table. The animation ring is set in a circular cutout so that it can be rotated through 360°, and there are calibrated sliding peg bars top and bottom. A field chart is used to select the required camera positions and is normally punched so that it can be pegged to either of the peg bars. Its centre represents the centre of the table at the zero setting of the bars.

The moves are plotted out on a sheet of semi-transparent paper also punched at the top or bottom (side pegging can also be used). The field sizes are drawn out in full and identified at the centre, AB, CD etc together with the relevant size, i.e. A 5 in B 10 in, etc. The length of the pan for all practical purposes is calculated from the centre of one field size to the centre of the next. Each shot key is identified with its own number as well as the shot number.

Calculating the speed of camera movements

The length of a move in time is often determined by its length in space — a 10 in pan normally takes longer than a 5 in pan if they are both to appear to be moving at the same speed. This is not always true, because the smaller the field size, the greater the apparent speed of any particular pan. For example, if the field size of the 5 in pan were exactly half that of the 10 in pan, both would appear to move at exactly the same speed if they took exactly the same time (number of frames). Although the first pan will travel twice as far as the second one *in space,* the difference between the field sizes makes them appear to move at equal speed. This is best understood if one thinks of two enlargements of the same photo — one twice the size of the other. By superimposing the pans over these photos we can see that the same area will be photographed in the same number of frames despite the difference of the field sizes to be used on each photograph — therefore the apparent speed of the two pans will be identical.

116

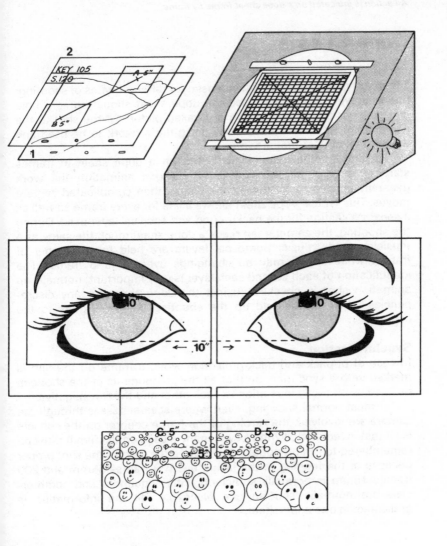

SHOT PLANNING

The animation table

Artwork (1) and Shot key (2) can be overlaid on the table. A cutout in the central
area of the disc corresponds to the backlight cutout on the animation stand table.
Here covered by a field size chart. The animation table also has its own backlight.

Relative speed of pans

Panning from A to B or from Ċ to D in the same number of frames produces the
same apparent speed because the distances are in proportion to the field sizes.
However, the visual effect of a pan is determined by the subject matter; a pan from
one eye to the other (A to B) in five seconds may appear slower than a 5 secs pan
over a crowd of people (C to D).

Dope Sheets

Different types of dope sheets are used for different types of shooting; but whatever the method used the dope sheet should be as simple and as clear as possible giving a detailed picture of the shot to the cameraman with clear indications as to the artwork to be used and the keys relating to that artwork.

The length of the shot is indicated on a dope sheet in frames starting at zero on the counter. In cartoon animation the work generally involves a lot more cel changes than complicated camera moves. This typical dope sheet allows a line for every frame as well as a separate section for the background and each cel layer used. During the shooting, the cameraman reads a dope sheet much the same as a musician reads music. Some cel layers are held for a number of frames while others may be changings every 2 or 3 frames The identification of each cel and each layer is very important; normally an animation shot is checked against the dope sheet for any discrepancies which might hold up the shooting, before it goes to the camera.

Synchronisation

In case of bi-pack and back-projection work, a frame on the film is marked with a sync mark so that all the components of the shot can be lined up correctly in relation to each other and the raw negative.

For most normal shooting, even where several passes through the camera are involved, the zeroing of the frame counter on the console is all that is required. (When a sync mark is used on the film it must be remembered to run off about 5 feet before the start of the shot proper because of the fogging in the lacing up; 100 frames 35mm and 200 frames 16mm is normally sufficient). Title sequences and commercials are normally shot in one piece, i.e. all the information is presented on one dope-sheet.

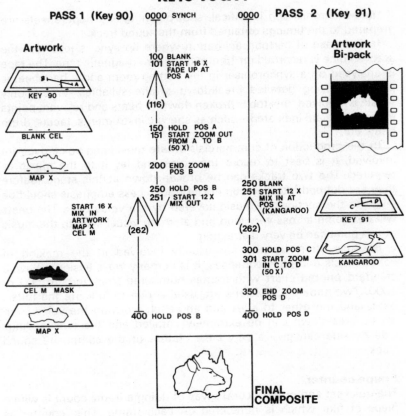

S.125
KEYS 90 & 91

PASS 1 (Key 90)   0000 SYNCH   0000   **PASS 2 (Key 91)**

Artwork

KEY 90

BLANK CEL

MAP X

START 16 X
MIX IN
ARTWORK
MAP X
CEL M

CEL M MASK

MAP X

Artwork Bi-pack

KEY 91

KANGAROO

100 BLANK
101 START 16 X
FADE UP AT
POS A

(116)

150 HOLD POS A
151 START ZOOM OUT
FROM A TO B
(50 X)

200 END ZOOM
POS B

250 HOLD POS B
251 START 12 X
MIX OUT

(262)

400 HOLD POS B

250 BLANK
251 START 12 X
MIX IN AT
POS C
(KANGAROO)

(262)

300 HOLD POS C
301 START ZOOM
IN C TO D
(50 X)

350 END ZOOM
POS D

400 HOLD POS D

FINAL COMPOSITE

PRODUCTION			SC	ANIMATOR		FTG				SHEET	

SOUND	ACTION	DIAL NOS	TOP				BOT	MOVES			DIAL NOS	FIELD	E	W	N	S	CAMERA INSTRUCTN
								BKGD	TOP	BOT							
		01									01						
		02									02						
		03									03						
		04									04						
		05									05						
		06									06						

ANIMATION

Typical cell dope sheet
All the camera instructions go on the dope sheet.

Timing

If the synchronisation is critical, shot planning and dope sheets are prepared to the timings obtained from the sound track.

In the case of cartoon animation where lip sync is involved, the actor's voice is recorded on 16 mm or 35 mm magnetic tape. The tape is analysed on a synchroniser in the cutting room and a bar sheet is prepared giving detailed breakdown of the syllables. Where only music is involved, this too is broken down to beats and relevant points in the music are indicated — such as specific instruments, tacets, drum beats etc.

In the production of commercials where music and voice over are involved, it is best to record the voice and lay it to the music as required. The two tracks can be broken down at this stage (before they are dubbed into one composite track). Less emphasis should be given to the sections of music covered by the voice over. The beats will not come across very loud and a strong visual sync to the music at this point can be very distracting.

Because short lengths are usually involved in the making of commercials and title sequences, it is in many ways easier to have a standard printed chart with frames numbered from zero to 500 or 1000. Two separate divisions are used — one to indicate the music beats and the other to start and end each word on the voice over. Music breakdown can be extremely detailed and the two readings side by side can give a very clear picture of the composite sound track.

Frame counter

The quickest and most accurate way of doing a frame count is with a piece of film which is numbered on each frame. This 'counter' is obtained by photographing the electronic frame counter from the console on the animation stand (phasing the camera motor so that it stops when the shutter is open and shooting continuously).

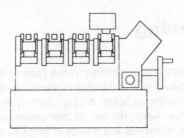

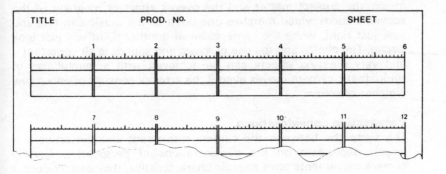

TITLE		PROD. N⁰.		SHEET	
FR.	MUSIC	COM.	FR.	MUSIC	COM.
1			51		
2			52		
3			53		
4			54		
5			55		
6			56		
7			57		
8			58		
9			59		
10			60		
11			61		
12			62		
13					

RELATING PICTURE TO SOUND

Motorised 'pic-syncs' are particularly useful for music and voice breakdowns. A pre-filmed counter gives frame by frame read-outs of the magnetic tracks. The read-outs can be prepared as rough guides for one track only or as very detailed transcript of several sound tracks including effects. They can take the form of horizontal bar sheets or vertical frame count. Sometimes the frames are divided into feet (Bars) and sometimes into seconds.

Shot Planning

The most important consideration in the planning of camera moves is to find a sympathetic relationship between the moves and the music or the moves and the subject matter, (artwork, stills etc.). A sharp focus pull can be said to be in sympathy with a sudden loud discordant sound, whereas the sweet chimes of a music box call for a long, gradual focus pull. Obviously also a lot depends on the type of music, the subject matter and the overall effect or meaning of the scene. A zoom which matches one point of the music can feel and look just right, while the same zoom at another point will just look wrong. The choice and the use of music and sounds is all important — and very pleasing effects can be achieved with a careful use of sympathetic camera moves even if the artwork consists of only a few blotches of colour.

Perspective considerations
The sympathy between the camera movement and the artwork is largely dependent on the considerations of perspective. Certain camera movements have specific characteristics; they can produce a specific effect of tilting or panning as in live action shooting. When such a move is used in conjunction with a scene containing the right perspective — the effect can be very convincing.

Very often the artwork is prepared deliberately using false perspective in one section of the drawing. The perspective can also be changed gradually during the shot so that a pan at a specific field size along such a drawing will appear as a 'live' pan where the camera pivots around a spot.

This kind of effect can also be achieved with still photographs, not only with specially designed artwork. A photograph is taken by a camera employing a tiny slit as shutter which scans the film while the lens rotates some 140°. A pan along such a photograph will appear realistic (at the correct field size).

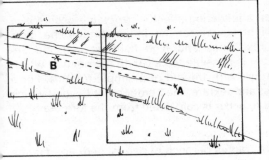

SHOT PLANNING

Camera movements must be in sympathy with the subject. For example, a pan
along a river; the pan is in sympathy with the river when the line of pan runs in the
same direction as the river with a gentle zoom matching the changing width.
Another is when a zoom to a smaller field size involves movement within the original
field size.
A vertical pan down the narrow street sets the mood without the perspective being
too clear at this field size. A sudden pull out (to position C) appears as though the
camera had been tilted down — due to the high-angle of the perspective.

Strobing

If the panning is too fast, a juddering effect – *strobing* – occurs at a point where persistence of vision can no longer bridge the gaps between the still pictures. Lines and high contrast subjects are particularly prone to this. It is possible to calculate the point at which the strobing becomes a risk with the aid of a simple formula. For a scene of average contrast and texture, the border point beyond which strobing can be expected to occur is calculated from the formula:

$$S = \frac{100}{f}$$

where S is the number of frames per inch of pan (speed) and f is the field size.

The contrast, shape and texture of the artwork vary so much that hard and fast rules are impossible. But in general, the higher the contrast, the greater the risk of strobing. With lettering, which is usually of very high contrast, the field size is not as important as the thickness of the lines. Further, the size of the screen can be a contributory factor to strobing. When projected on a large cinema screen a scene may appear to strobe while the same scene may be perfectly all right on a TV screen.

Strobing in moving artwork
Strobing also occurs in animated movement if the movements are too great. This can be cured by painting more in-between moves. If this is not possible, the in-between cels are smeared using the 'dry brush' technique so that the image is no longer clear and sharp.

Whip pans
Sometimes the strobing is used deliberately to give a specific effect; this is usually in the form of a very quick pan or *whip (swish) pan.* Alternatively to avoid strobing the shutter speed can be lengthened; and the shot made continuously as the table is moved the required distance. This gives a smeared (blurred) effect, adding to the realism.

Zooms
Strobing is not normally a problem with the zoom, unless a pan is also involved. However, there is a great danger of a shot using both pan and zoom movements strobing at the smaller field size end of the move and not strobing during the rest of the shot.

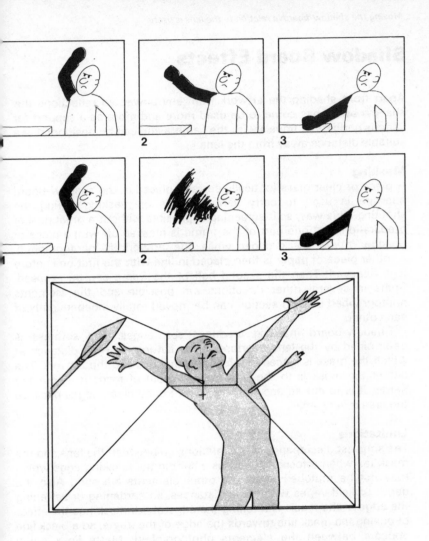

FAST MOVEMENTS

Dry-brush technique is used to give a blurred image to the in-between cels when the speed of the action is likely to make it strobe.

Crash zooms can have great impact, especially when the centres of the two field-sizes are close.

125

Shadow Board Effects

Apart from shading the artwork from any unwanted reflections the shadow board has come to be used more and more as a support for various gadgets. It travels with the camera and can be positioned at a suitable distance away from the lens.

Masking

A piece of clear glass (optically correct) placed in the shadow-board aperture is used to carry various types of masking during the shooting. This way, split-screening is possible without a great deal of preparation, e.g. one part of the frame is masked off with a piece of opaque, *matte* black paper while the artwork is photographed. Another piece of paper is then placed in line with the first one before it is removed. Then the second half of the frame can be exposed. Splits in several other directions are possible and the elements photographed in each section can be moved totally independently of each other.

Shadow-board masking produces soft edges. The softness is determined by the lens aperture, focus setting, and the distance at which the mask is placed in relation to the lens and the artwork. The nearer the mask is to the lens the more out of focus it is, but the harder it is to cut an accurate mask with good clean edges because the area is very small.

Limitations

The smallest discrepancy in the relationship between the lens and the mask (as when refocusing) causes a shift in the masking edge which may not be matched when the other elements are shot. Also the depth of field varies with focus distances, so hardening or softening the edge of the mask. Hardening the edge of the mask has the effect of pulling the mask line towards the edge of the frame, so a black line appears between the elements photographed. Matte lines going through the lens centre can generally accommodate greater changes in field sizes.

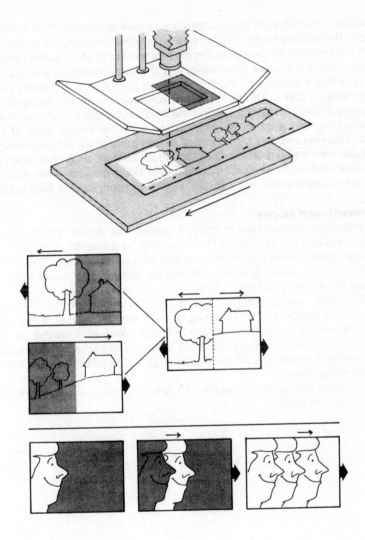

THE SHADOW BOARD

Split-screen can be done quickly and effectively with a matte and counter matte on the shadow board.
The splitting does not have to follow any specific geometric pattern; the outline may be suggested by the shape of the object in the picture.
The same image can be multiplied several times, each repeat appearing to move out from behind or out of the first image.

127

Shadow Board – Wipes

A static matte line on the shadow board can also be used as a static wipe. The required section of the map (or other artwork) is masked off and the panning move along the map executed. With a counter matte in position, the same background, and the same exposure are used to inlay a blank section of the frame which contains background only. This is done static. The matte line is not visible over the background (as this is the same) and the outline of a land mass (or whatever the subject matter) appears to materialise with the progression of the pan. This method can also be used to add body to an outlined image, but the camera pass with the outline must be done as a matching pan as well as having identical background. The technique may also be used to superimpose small details, such as a route outline on a map.

Conventional wipes

A soft-edge matte line is moved across the frame progressively obscuring one scene. This is then matched by a counter matte on the second pass, revealing another scene at the same rate. The frame area (at the shadow board level) can be divided into equal parts to give a smooth wipe of any length.

A device, using worm-screw drive, can be made to ensure a smooth movement of the masks (masks are pegged to a separate peg-bar which is attached to a thin metal plate, and moved up and down by the nut travelling along the screw). The same considerations regarding the softness of the matte edge apply as in the case of the static matte lines.

The direction and the shape of both the static and conventional wipes can be varied.

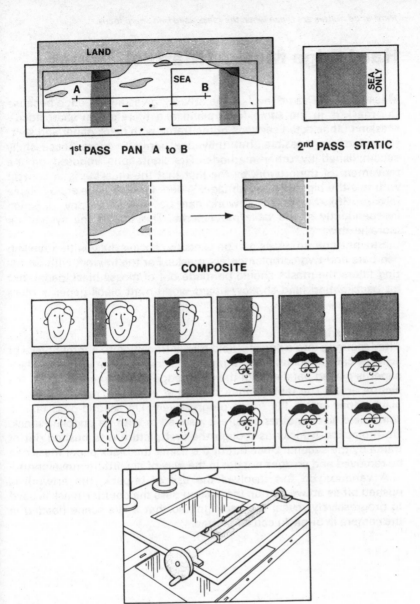

1st PASS PAN A to B

2nd PASS STATIC

COMPOSITE

WIPES

Wipes with fixed matte
With the shadow-board matte fixed, the sea shore artwork is panned. Then with the countermatte sea only is printed in to the space so land appears to materialise from the sea as the pan continues.

Moving matte
Conventional soft-edged wipes can be executed on the shadow board with the help of a pegbar attached to a worm-screw drive on the shadow board.

T.A.S.—I

Hard Edge Masks (Mattes), Wipes

Masking at the same level as the artwork gives a hard edge because the mask is in the same focal plane and therefore in sharp focus. Masking off selected sections of the frame with black paper and split-screening are possible, but they are normally more successfully accomplished by other methods. The limitations imposed on the movement of the artwork by the fact that the masking is in contact with it is the biggest disadvantage. Where floating pegs are available (see p. 56), masks or artwork can be moved in any direction independently of the table movements. This makes the system far more flexible.

Straightforward wipes can be executed successfully with travelling peg bars and two complementary masks. For top lit work with polarizing filters the masks should be made out of glossy black paper, but for backlighting (and shadow-board work) matt black paper is more suitable.

Push-off wipe

After zooming into a specific field size, a transition to another piece of artwork can be achieved by a push-off wipe. A piece of glossy black paper is placed parallel with the outer edge of the frame (outside the picture area). The table is then panned at a specific rate, so that the black paper enters the frame progressively. On second pass (at the same field size) another picture is panned in with an opposite mask. On projection it looks as though the first picture was pushed out of frame by the second. Once out of the frame the black paper mask can be removed and so does not get in the way of any future movements.

A variation on this involves the use of bi-pack; the artwork is pushed off as above, but on the second pass the counter-mask is used to progressively reveal the backlight, so that a live scene (loaded in the camera in bi-pack) can be printed.

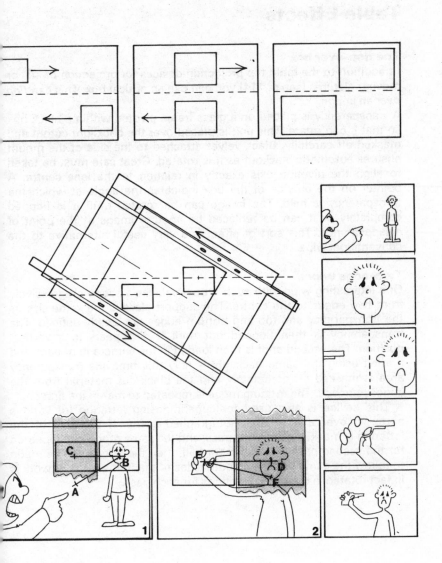

HARD EDGE EFFECTS

Using two separate scenes

Separate pieces of artwork can be made to follow different moves when shot
against a black background, if care is taken to avoid overlaps.
Some wipes and similar effects can be done on the table in one pass. For diagonal
movements rotation is set to a suitable angle.

The push-off wipe

A push-off wipe enables one scene (1) to be pushed out of the screen area by
another (2).

Table Effects

The flop-over box

In addition to the table top projection devices for projection of still or moving pictures (see p. 114) you can use an optical box. This can *flop over* an image.

A transparency is placed on a glass frame pivoted within a black box so that it can rotate. This unit is placed over the backlight cutout and masked off carefully. Black velvet attached to the side of the mount ensures automatic blackout as it is rotated. Great care must be taken to align the pivoting axis exactly in relation to the lens centre. A pointer on the outside of the box indicates the angle at which the transparency is held. The image can be rotated until it is flopped completely or it can be replaced by another image at the point of disappearence. This sort of effect is a very useful alternative to the conventional wipe.

Two-edge wipes

One interesting wipe with such a box replaces a scene progressively from two edges to the centre. The support glass is the same size as the transparency and top and bottom edges are clearly defined. The transparency is then flopped out until it disappears in a vertical position. The second shot is then loaded in the camera in bi-pack and printed using the same backlight – only this time the transparency area is masked off completely and the black-out material from the edges removed. The rotating move is repeated to match the first one.

This device is also used for superimposing lettering (or various patterns) over a normally photographed scene. If one half of the lettering is masked off for one pass, and the same procedure repeated for the second pass with the other half, then the letters can be made to follow the same pattern on both sides of the frame – the artwork is in fact rotated in opposite directions for each pass.

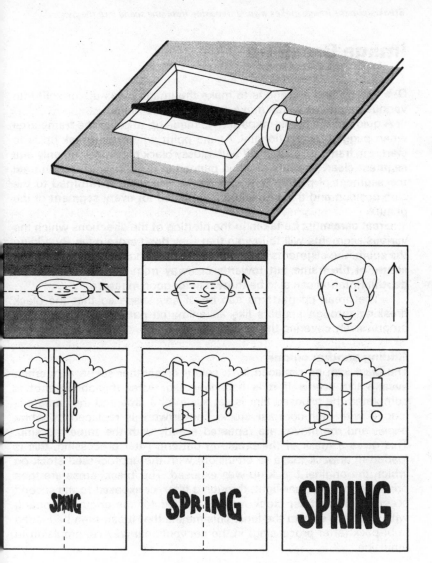

THE FLOP BOX

A simple box for rotating material through measured angles has many uses.
Horizontal flop of the whole image can be made with the use of a flop-box and a
transparency.
Flopping superimposed titles over a normal scene adds to the three dimensional
effect.
By masking off one half of the frame at a time identical effects can be achieved for
both halves of the title.

Image Break up

One way to end a scene is to make the image break up, or split into various fragments which move in different directions.

A guide of the break-up pattern is made up to cover the frame area when pegged conventionally. At the point where the break up is to start, the frame is masked off with glossy black paper leaving only one segment clear. The table is then panned in the chosen direction until the segment of picture is out of frame. The table is returned to the zero position and this procedure is repeated for every segment of the picture.

Great care must be taken in the plotting of the directions which the various segments will follow so that they don't cross over. By adding the zoom, the segments can be made to move not only away from the centre of the frame but towards or away from the camera also (in depth). Rotation can also be thrown in for good measure.

The break up patterns can be of any shape so that the black breaking through appears like an animated pattern which expands progressively covering the whole frame.

Adding another colour

The black can be replaced by a colour or another scene altogether, even a live scene, if it is backprojected. After the above shot is completed the exposed film is set aside for a time and the camera is loaded with high-contrast stock. The artwork is replaced by white paper, and the moves are repeated exactly with the same masking. This gives a mask of the break-up pattern. After processing, this is loaded in bi-pack (base to emulsion) with the unprocessed stock on which the original break up was exposed. The 'black' areas are then printed either on clear-light, through a filter, or exposed to the second scene. High-contrast stock may be loaded for the original shooting with the base side to the lens. This means that it can then be loaded in bi-pack (after processing) in the conventional way i.e. emulsion to emulsion.

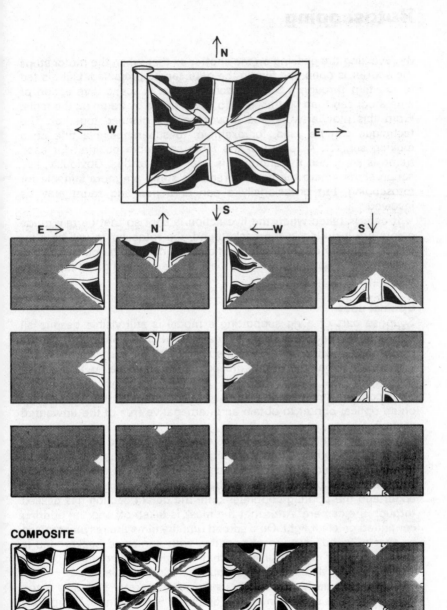

IMAGE BREAK-UP

A guide is made first to determine the shape.

Each segment is shot on a separate pass through the camera while the others are masked off. By careful application of zoom and rotation the segments can be made to spin or float in depth.

Rotoscoping

By reversing the phasing on the shutter so that when the motor stops the shutter is open, the film in the gate can be projected. Light is fed to the film through a 90° rotoscope prism. A scene (live action or animated) can then be traced onto paper frame by frame on the table. From this plot, artwork and moves can be planned together. The technique can be used, for example, to superimpose a title on a moving subject. A record of the table and zoom position for each frame is kept, and the shooting is later done to this. Obviously, live action shots where the camera remains static are more suitable for rotoscoping, but occasionally a pan or a pan and zoom may be involved.

If care is taken when the live action is shot so that certain guide points are included in the background, the rotoscoping will be a lot easier. Sometimes small white reticles (marks) can be placed on the background – particularly when they can be masked off in the marry up stage.

Special uses

Suppose part of a rig supporting a model is still visible despite all efforts in the shooting stage to mask it off. The entire shot can be rotoscoped and the position of the rig plotted for every frame. A soft edge matte is painted to the rotoscoped shape of the rig, and is then shot with the table retracing all the positions obtained by rotroscoping. This mask is then used in contact with the interpositive on an optical printer to obtain an internegative free of the unwanted section.

The most common defect in live action is when the boom operator drops the microphone into the shot; this can be eliminated simply by printing the interpositive of the scene in bi-pack; at the appropriate frame a mask is placed across the backlight (out of focus to give a soft edge) and the printing continues until the defect section has passed through the camera. After that the mask is taken off and the printing continued on clear light. On a serond run, the films are resynchronised so that a "good" section of negative with unmarred background is used. A counter matte is used so that the good background is printed into the previously masked area. Thus the scene is repaired.

This technique is particularly useful when normal shooting is too dangerous, e.g. scenes involving actors & wild animals; explosions very close to the actor etc.

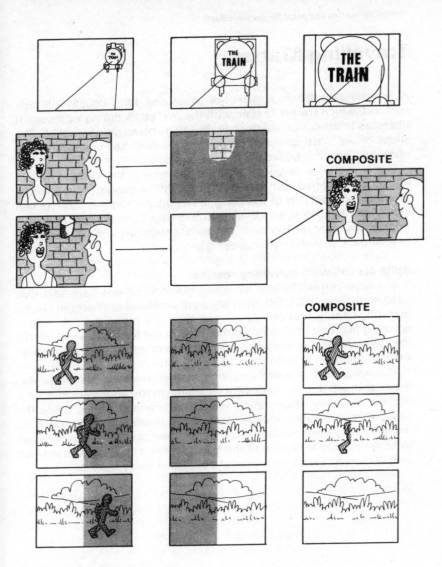

MATTES AND ROTOSCOPE

A live action scene is rotoscoped to draw guide points so that captions can be animated to fit.

Repairing defects
A section from the good part of the scene is used to repair the same section a few frames apart.

Altering live action
Using a similar technique, two parts of one shot may be superimposed; so that for example, a man disappears through an invisible line in an unbroken background.

Travelling Mattes

A travelling matte is a piece of processed film, usually of high contrast, which travels in sync with the raw stock during exposure. It obscures (mattes out) sections of the image being photographed. The shape of the matte depends on the image which had previously been photographed to produce the travelling matte.

If the matte is to go in with the raw stock, the camera should ideally be equipped with a bi-pack magazine. However, it is possible to wind short lengths of travelling matte on the same roll as the raw stock, but this must be done with extreme caution. The travelling mattes may alternatively go in the aerial image projector, either singly or in bi-pack with the material being projected.

Split-screen with travelling mattes

The image carried by the travelling matte does not have to move itself, it is often static. For example a conventional split-screen can be made by filming first one scene and then the other through mattes covering first one half and then the other of the frame. Pairs of mattes can be made in any shape or size, and are normally distinguished as *male* and *female,* or simply *matte* and *counter-matte.*

The advantage of using travelling mattes for static split-screening is not so much the accuracy with which the matte edges are matched, but the flexibility of operation which this method offers. Since the artwork is completely independent of the matte, not only can it be moved in any direction but it can be reduced or enlarged as required to fit the particular section of the frame where it is being inserted — by simply moving the camera closer to or farther away from it.

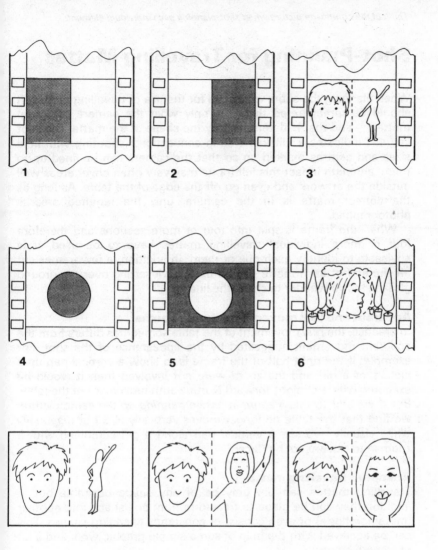

TRAVELLING MATTE SHOTS

Matte (1) and counter-matte (2) are used on successive passes to combine two or more parts to one scene.

Perhaps the greatest advantage of split-screening with travelling mattes is that it enables different movements to be made in each part, including zooms.

Shot-Planning for Travelling Mattes

When planning the shots which call for the use of travelling mattes, it should be remembered that it is only what the camera sees that matters – and that is determined by the shape of the matte. The shot key still indicates a full frame as in conventional shooting with field sizes and centres marked up so that the camera can be lined up to them, although in fact this full frame may very often cover areas well outside the artwork and even go off the edge of the table. As long as the correct matte is in the camera, only the required area is photographed.

When the frame is split into four or more sections and therefore four or more individual travelling mattes have to be used, it is advisable to identify each one of them. In addition, a few frames cut off the end of each matte can be used for inserting over the ground glass in the viewfinder to check the line up.

Apparent and real movements during zooms

In practice, the *real* movement of the table sometimes differs from the apparent movement suggested by the appearance of the shot. For example: if the right half of the frame is to show a vertical pan up a picture of a girl and the zoom were not involved then it would be executed with a straight-forward North/South movement of the table. But if we add to this a *zoom in* while *panning up* the same picture, we find that the table no longer moves vertically N/S but *diagonally* while visually, we see a vertical pan along a girl combined with a zoom in to close-up of her face.

Animated travelling matte

Travelling mattes can not only be of any shape desirable but in addition they can be made to transform from one shape into another (metamorphosis) or even consist of constantly changing shapes. This can be achieved with the help of some simple graphic work and a lot of camera moves.

You can make a much more fluid type of travelling matte by cel animation. The changing shapes of the matte are painted in subtle progression. A counter-matte can also be painted at the same time or it can be derived by making a positive or negative print (as the case may be) from the first matte.

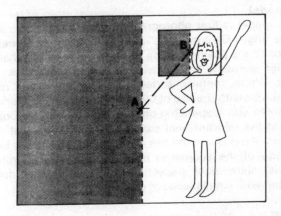

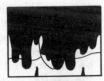

ANIMATED MATTES

Zooms
Although the pan up appears to be vertical during this zooming split-screen shot,
the shot plan indicates that in fact the table is panning *diagonally*.

Animated titles
A sequence of animation cels are photographed on Hi-contrast stock to produce a
travelling matte and counter-matte. The matte is used to mask out part of the
scene, the counter-matte for clear light printing. With filters this can be coloured.

141

The illusion of travel in depth is most effective against a static or gently panning background.

Space Shots

One exciting part of animation stand travelling matte work is the realistic portrayal of spaceships or rockets travelling through space. This can be done with self-matting positive and a male matte to act as counter-matte.

Using a model
A realistic model is first photographed with a still camera from the appropriate angle. Care must be taken in lighting the model so that it corresponds to the position of the sun and the light and shadow areas of the other elements to be included in the same shot, i.e. Earth, Moon, etc. White, metallic surfaces of spaceships and rockets are best reproduced with the use of black-and-white stills. A print is made to the required size (depending on how big or small the object needs to appear at the relevant field sizes). A bigger image will give better reproduction of detail and the risk of a visible matte-line is less.

The image of the subject is then cut out. The rostrum table is covered with shiny black paper, and the cutout stuck down in the right position with small pieces of double sided tape.

Movement
The illusion of movement is created by zooming or panning the camera. This illusion is reinforced when the shot is inlayed into a suitable static or counter-moving background.

Great care must be taken when planning a shot of this kind that the object appears to move along its natural line of travel. It should also be remembered that zooming in pulls an off-centre subject away from the centre. It is best to plan shots so that the travelling or flying objects do not have to cross the horizontal and vertical centre lines. If they do, then a special panning move has to be worked out taking into account the pulling effect of the zoom and compensating for it. In addition, if the pan can be done with the use of only one movement the risk of inaccuracy during the actual shooting is diminished.

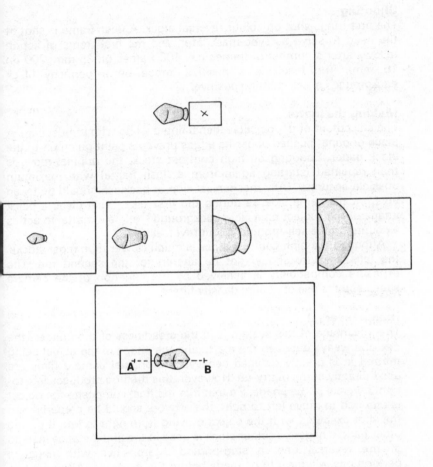

SPACE SHOTS

If a rocket is facing left and is positioned just left of the frame centre at the widest field size, it will appear to travel towards the camera and exit out of frame on the left when only the ZOOM is used, without any panning.

By contrast if the same rocket is in the same position in the screen but is facing right and is required to exit right of frame in much the same way as before we find that a great deal of E/W panning is necessary to accomplish this. Furthermore if this panning distance is simply divided into equal increments for each frame (to correspond to the zoom) the resulting shot appears very strange, i.e. the object is hardly moving at all at first and then it accelerates rapidly and disappears out of the frame.

143

Space Shots 2

Shooting
The first run is shot on colour reversal stock. A flash frame is shot at the head to serve as sync-mark later, and the first frame of action follows after a number of frames (i.e. 100 frames on 35 mm; 200 on 16 mm). The result is a positive image on a perfectly black background i.e. self-matting positive.

Making the matte
The still cutout of the object is then painted white with utmost care. A piece of paper pushed under its edges prevents paint going on to the black paper. Shooting on high contrast stock, the original move is then repeated (starting again from a flash frame) with maximum possible accuracy. (Any mechanical slop or backlash should be taken up from the same side as during the first take.) This gives a black image of the subject on a clear background – a 'male matte' to act as a counter to the self-matting colour reversal shot.

Although the high contrast stock is much slower than most stocks, the lens aperture should not be altered for the second run. The exposure compatibility is achieved by the variation of the camera speed and the use of neutral density filters.

Image reversal
The advantage of this system is in the steadiness of the images; the risk of a weave between the matte and the image of the object being matted in is greatly reduced because the original camera films are used directly in the marry-up. However, this method produces left-to-right reversal of the image. So that if in the final composite the object is required to move left to right, the artwork should be prepared and the shot executed with the object moving from right to left. If on the other hand a negative colour stock is used in the first instance instead of the reversal one, a step-printed interpositive with negative perforations will have to be made before the marry-up. Although this gives the correct left to right reproduction of the image, the geometry of the counter-matte is wrong. So it has to be used base-to-emulsion instead of the emulsion-to-emulsion with the raw stock. To avoid this, you can load the high contrast stock with base to lens for the original shooting, or make an intermediate on reversal stock and print the matte from that.

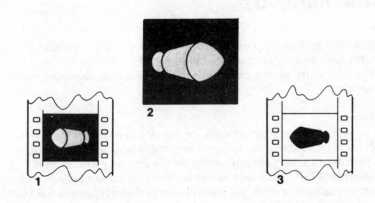

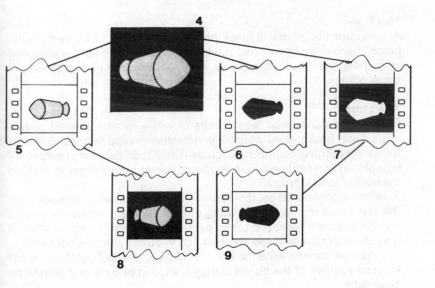

ELEMENTS OF INSERTING A ROCKET

Simple mattes

The image is flopped left to right (mirror-like) in the marry-up if mattes are shot directly.
1, Original cutout on black background. 2, Colour reversal self-matting image. 3, Hi-con negative counter-matte (male) image of the white-painted original.

Avoiding image reversal

4, Original cutout on black BG. 5, Colour negative. 6, Hi-con negative matte – incompatible with the interpositive. 7, B/W (or colour) reversal of the white painted original. 8, Interpositive. 9, Male matte – compatible with interpositive.

The Marry-Up

When the self-matting colour reversal and the high contrast counter matte have been processed, the shot can then be married up with the other elements of the composite picture such as the stars, planets, Sun, etc.

Planets
It is best to use transparencies for planets and other celestial bodies where the colour and texture are important. All the background elements may be panning gently as though they are all made up of one picture but are in fact all separate elements of varying sizes. The panning speeds of each are interrelated to their respective field sizes.

The atmospheric haze around planets with atmosphere such as Earth is obtained by putting gauze filters in front of the lens.

The Sun
A circle cut out of matte black paper with a piece of frosted plastic placed behind it gives a most realistic sun effect. The flare is obtained by overexposing by 8 stops more than is needed for a normal back-lit transparency.

The stars
Shiny black paper with small drops of white paint scattered over it gives a star background which is very realistic in appearance. It is best to use very strong polarizers (such as H.N. 22) so that the stars can be brought up in brightness (overexposed) without the danger of making the background lighter.

In the marry-up stage, the counter-matte is carried in bi-pack with the raw stock during the shooting of each element where the object (in this case the rocket) crosses over that element. In some shots it may travel across only one element and in others across all of them.

When all other elements are married up, the self-matting colour reversal positive of the object is then loaded in bi-pack and printed on clear light.

A particular advantage of this method is that the pair of travelling mattes so obtained can be married-up into any number of different backgrounds.

THE MARRY-UP

All the elements are added together to make a realistic space shot. Stars, Sun, foreground, Earth and rocket are all prepared separately.

Adding Live Action

By using a specially adapted 16 mm projector on the artwork table, and by raising the focus plane, it is possible to add live-action material for example in the windows of the spaceship. The procedure is exactly the same as described above except that the self-matting colour reversal positive is done with two passes through the camera. For the first pass, the windows of the spaceship are cut out so that only black paper can be seen in their place. On the second pass the black paper in the window area is removed to reveal the live material back-projected. The rest of the procedure is unaltered.

Interpositive/internegative
When the live action element, such as the pilots in the cockpit of a spaceship, constitutes a large part of the total composite scene, any deterioration in the quality of the live image is critical. Here it is best to use interpositive – internegative procedures.

The cutout of the spaceship is stuck on the glass in a static position. The interpositive of the background action is loaded in bi-pack with the internegative (raw stock); this then is printed on clear light with the cutout of the spaceship acting as a matte (windows are also blacked out).

On the second pass the interpositive of the live action inserts for the windows are printed through the window areas only with the rest of the table blacked out. The live action must have been shot to the right size in the first place so that it fits the window areas. It is often possible to prepare an interpositive to fit the desired part of the frame by optical printing. The third pass involves a straightforward photograph of the spaceship cutout lit from above with its windows and the rest of the frame area blacked out.

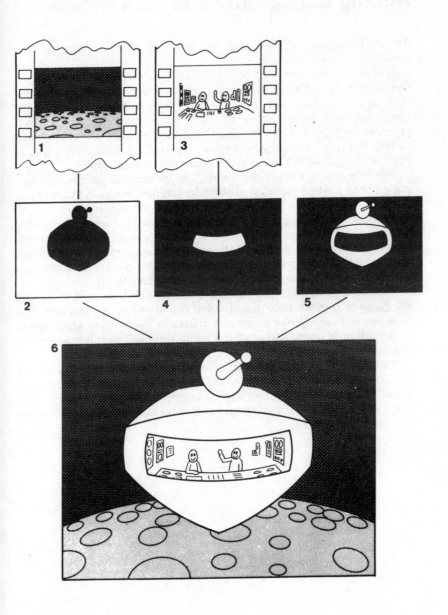

INSERTING LIVE ACTION INTO ANIMATED SCENES

Combining suitable shots with travelling mattes adds realism.
1, Interpositive background action. 2, Cutout of spacecraft lit from behind (windows masked off). 3, Interpositive of live action to be inserted into cockpit. 4, Windows of the cutout left clear; surrounding area masked off. 5, Cutout of the spacecraft – top-lit (windows masked off). 6, The composite picture.

Adding Backgrounds to Live Action

An animation stand can also be used to add sections to the background in a live scene.

The set for a static shot of a ballroom with elaborate ceiling and chandeliers is not only too costly to build but would present the lighting cameraman with a lot of difficulties (the lights are usually supported by a gantry above the set). So, although the chandeliers can still be real (if they are suspended low enough) the rest of the ceiling will most certainly be painted (matted in). Sometimes this is done on the actual set to avoid the necessity for duplication.

The live scene (minus the ceiling) is rotoscoped (projected) and traced onto a white material suitable for painting which is stuck to the glass on the rostrum table. The artist takes his guidelines from the rotoscoped image and paints in the ceiling taking care to match the colours of the original scene. He then cuts a line along useful points where the projected and the painted scenes overlap and the bottom section is then removed from the glass, leaving a clear area through which the original scene can be printed using backlights.

On the second pass, top lights are used (with black velvet behind the glass to prevent reflections) — and the marry-up is complete. The new painted ceiling has acted as a matte in the printing stage when backlighting is used, and is at the same time self-matting when the top-lighting is used.

This method is of particular advantage when very large sets are required which would be very costly or even impossible to build, such as for example, where actors appear very small in giant settings. Only the areas where the actors stand need to be built as real sets — all the rest can be painted in.

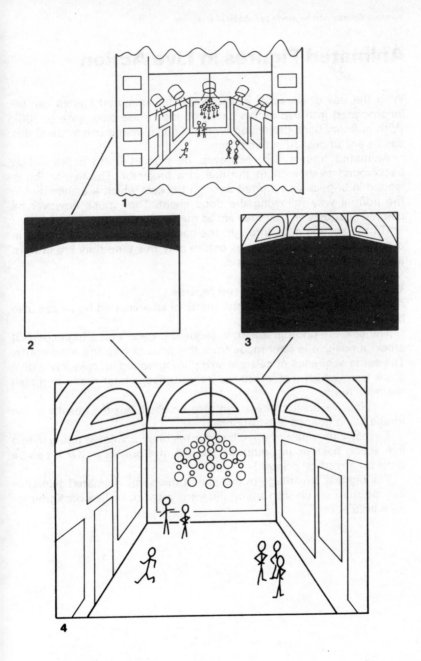

OTHER SCENES

1, Interpositive of live action scene. 2, Painted matte lit from behind. 3, Painted matte lit from above. 4, Composite.

Adding backgrounds is not confined to space shots. It can reduce the cost of magnificent studio sets, such as ballrooms, without the need for in-camera mattes or glass shots.

151

Animated Figures in Live Action

With the use of an aerial image projector, animated figures can be incorporated into live action backgrounds in one pass. (see p. 106). With ordinary back-projection (without aerial image condensers) this can be accomplished in two passes.

Animated figures can, however, be matted in to a live action background even without the use of a projector. The live action is loaded in bi-pack and printed through the cels which are animated in the normal way following the dope sheet. They must, however be painted opaquely so that they act as mattes for printing.

On the second pass through the camera the cels are animated in exactly the same sequence as before only this time they are lit from above, with a black background.

Travelling mattes of animated figures

A travelling matte and a counter matte of an animated figure can also be obtained in this way.

The cels are photographed, in sequence, backlit on a high contrast stock; a positive is later made from this print to give the male matte. The same sequence of cels are also photographed on colour negative stock from which a step-printed interpositive is later made to match the male matte.

A colour reversal process can also be used, but this results in the image being flopped left-to-right.

To marry up a pair of travelling mattes of an animated figure in to a live action background requires the use of a projector. (Or it can be done on an optical printer.)

The biggest advantage of this is that this same animated sequence can be married up into many different artwork or live backgrounds with little effort.

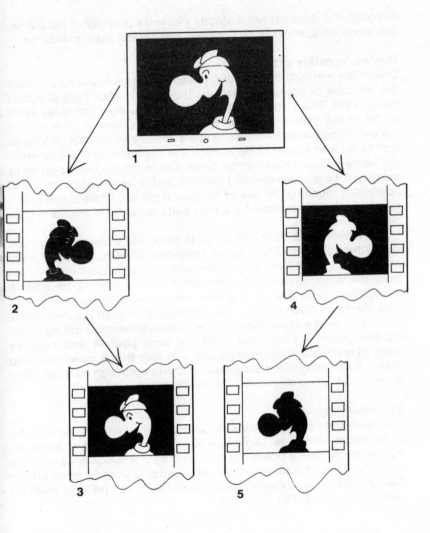

MAKING TRAVELLING MATTES

If you want to add them to live action, you can make the mattes from your
animated characters.
1, Original artwork (animation cel on black background). 2, Colour negative. 3,
Interpositive. 4, Hi-con negative from same artwork – backlit. 5, Hi-con
positive – male matte (counter matte to the interpositive image).

153

Live Action and Animated Backgrounds

Although this does not come strictly within the province of the animation stand work, a lot can be achieved with careful experimentation.

Mattes from live action

One of the methods of obtaining travelling mattes of live figures uses the principle of colour separation. The actor is shot against a blue background. This colour is usually chosen because it can most easily be taken out from a scene without causing an unacceptable shift in the overall colour balance. Any primary colour can be used, as long as it does not also appear in the wardrobe or the make up of the artists.

The travelling mattes can be derived from the original negative by means of colour separation positives and a series of complicated operations requiring the use of an optical printer. There is however a relatively simpler method by which quite acceptable results can be obtained.

The master positive is printed on to black-and white panchromatic stock, through a blue filter to give a negative with a black background, and through a red filter to give one with a clear background. A print from the latter (or reversal processing) gives a positive on a black background. Both this and the blue filter negative are printed in turn onto the same piece of high contrast stock. The result is a completely black area in the exact shape of the subject (covering both light and shadow areas — hence the need for both positive and negative separations) on a clear background — in fact it is a male travelling matte. By printing the male travelling matte onto high contrast stock a female travelling matte (counter matte) is obtained.

The marry-up

The animated scene can either be photographed directly through the male matte which is carried in bi-pack with the raw stock, or separately so that a positive is prepared from it which is used in the marry up. The counter matte (female matte) is used to mask off the background of the original master positive, when printing (with an aerial image projector).

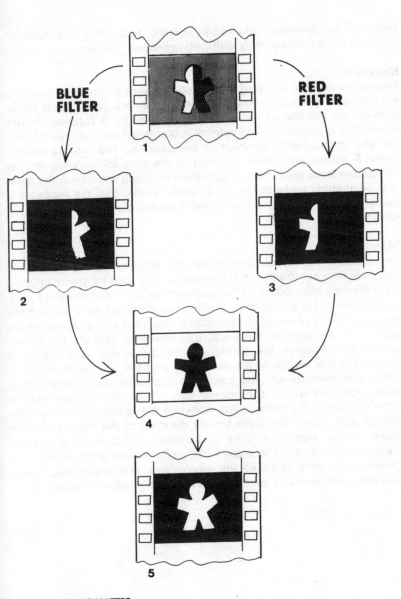

MAKING TRAVELLING MATTES

1, Original positive in colour with blue background. 2, B and W negative image printed through a blue filter. 3, B and W positive image printed through a red filter (processed as reversal). 4, High contrast negative onto which both 2 and 3 have been printed. 5, Counter matte made from 4.

A live action subject can be used to prepare mattes if photographed against a suitable coloured background. Blue is most commonly used.

Some really way-out effects can be produced this way.

Slit-Scan

This method produces geometric shapes from varied patterns of colour or even forms grossly distorted live-action scenes.

Exposure

Through a slit (or a series of slits), coloured light traces patterns on to a frame of film which is held static in the camera gate. This is made possible by the use of two separate shutters (or a capping shutter where this is available). The camera motor is set so that it stops with the film in the taking position in the gate and the camera shutter open. A secondary shutter in front of the lens (or capping shutter behind the lens) prevents the light from reaching the film in the gate. It is by opening and closing this auxiliary shutter that the exposure is made. A simple solenoid motor and a cable release can do this job efficiently.

Movements

The camera travels up and down the column during the actual exposure for each frame, so the exposure time can be anything up to 30 or 40 secs (depending on the length of track and speed used.)

The solenoid is activated by a micro-switch attached to the camera mount. A piece of metal shaped into an inverted V is attached to the column at the start of the track; this serves to activate the micro-switch and so open the shutter. At the other end of the track it operates a trip switch in the same way and the shutter is closed. A frame has been taken. The camera motor is used to move a new frame into position in the normal way whilst the auxiliary shutter remains closed. As the camera moves in the opposite direction, the shutter will open, stay open for the duration of the track and close again at the end of it. This is obviously a laborious and time-consuming task, but the results can make it well worthwhile. It is, however, possible to make the whole operation automatic, though this is best done with a specially built horizontally travelling set-up.

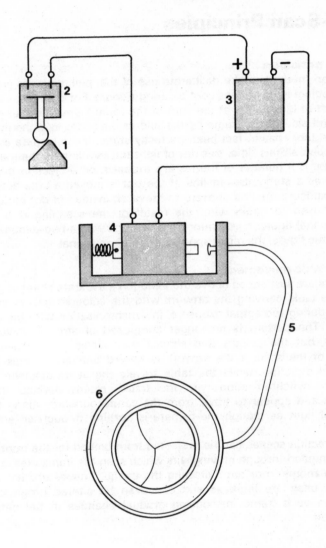

SLIT-SCAN MECHANISM

For this system the shutter must be held open for measured length of time. If there
is no capping shutter, a separate shutter can be fitted in front of the lens. Set at B
(bulb exposure) this shutter can be operated by a simple solenoid system.
1, Trigger. 2, Micro-switch. 3, Battery. 4, Solenoid (spring loaded). 5, Cable release.
6, Shutter mechanism.

It is possible to predict the shape of the pattern.

Slit–Scan Principles

Visual principles
Slit-scan methods make deliberate use of the 'pull' which is created on an object lying off lens centre during a zoom. For example, a dot of light left of lens centre at the start of the zoom in, moves over to the left hand side of the frame by the end of the zoom in, although the rostrum table has in fact been perfectly static. If the camera shutter stays open all this time, this dot of light traces a line on the frame in the gate. If a number of frames are exposed, on projection this will appear as a static straight line. If the dot is moved a little between each exposure the line appears to move. If, instead of dot of light, a line is used to begin with, the result of the scanning is a two-dimensional figure. Furthermore, if one starts with a two-dimensional geometric figure, the result appears three-dimensional.

Using table movements
The slits are suspended above the table (on a separate sheet of glass) and the table carrying the artwork with the coloured gels is moved slowly during the actual exposure, in synchronisation with the zoom (track). The pattern is no longer composed of streaks of various colours, but the colours and shapes themselves change over the length of the scan. If the artwork is moved between frames in an outward direction, while the table travels the same distance each time (in synchronisation with the track), clearly defined shapes emerge and appear to travel from the centre outwards along these walls of light as though the camera is hurtling through an endless tunnel.

Live action scenes can be projected from behind (or the front) and photographed through moving slits which scan the frame area, as the camera zooms in or out distorting the image. Shapes of slits which can be used are limitless and can even be altered progressively between each frame introducing gradual changes in the patterns produced.

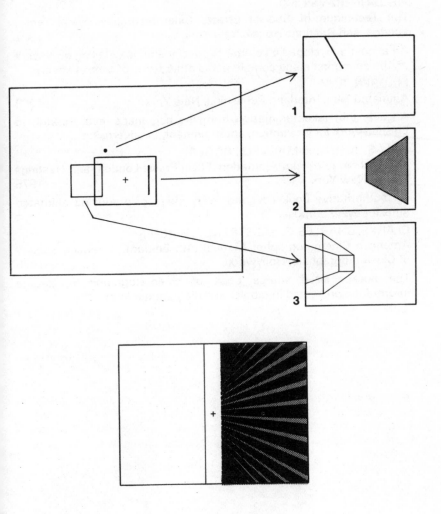

SLIT-SCAN EFFECTS

Shape and lines
Scanning various shapes produces different effects. The results are achieved by
zooming from one field size to the other. 1, A dot becomes a line. 2, A line becomes
a shape. 3, A shape appears to gain a third dimension.
Two colour static slit with static background.

159

Further Reading

FIELDING, RAYMOND:
The Technique of Special Effects Cinematography. Focal Press, London, and Hastings House, New York 1972

An almost encyclopedic volume of special effects detailing how work on the animation stand complements other types of special effects.

MADSEN, ROY:
Animated Film, Interland Publishing, New York 1969

A guide that takes animation from the beginner's level through to finished work for instruction, entertainment, or advertising.

HALAS, JOHN and MANVELL, ROGER:
The Technique of Film Animation. Focal Press, London, and Hastings House, New York 1976

An authoritative book covering every stage of producing animated films for every purpose.

CLARKE, CHARLES G. and STRENGE, WALTER:
American Cinematographer Manual (4th Edition). American Society of Cinematographers, Hollywood 1975

The pocket sized source book of cinematographic up-to-date information presented in tabular and diagramatic form.

Glossary

Academy Aperture (28) The opening in a 35mm camera or projector gate defined by the United States Academy of Motion Pictures Arts and Sciences. Smaller than the maximum frame area (see **Full Aperture**) and shifted to one side it leaves room for an optical sound track.

Aerial Image (106) (108) An optical system enabling the camera to photograph a backprojected scene via condensers set in the table; animation cels placed over the condensers can be photographed simultaneously with the back projected scene.

Angle The viewpoint of an observer i.e. the camera, which dictates the perspective in laying out a scene.

Animation (10) (152) (154) The art of giving apparent movement in inanimate objects or a series of drawings.

Animation Cycle (12) A series of drawings or cels which can be photographed over and over to give the illusion of a continuous, repeatitive action.

Animation Table (18) The table onto which the artwork is placed for filming; it can be rotated and moved in any direction and equipped with moving peg bars for panning the artwork independently. Artists' animation table is a simplified version of the shooting table; and in its simplest form it is a drawing board with a backlit area and a fixed registration peg bar; and more sophisticated ones have movements available, to assist shot planning.

Aperture (34) A variable lens opening which controls the intensity of light reaching the film. (See also **Iris, Camera Aperture, Projector Aperture**).

A.S.A. Speed (94) Speed arithmetic system defined by the American National Standards Distribution used for rating the sensitivity to light (speed) of photographic emulsions.

Auto-Focus (32) System which keeps the camera lens focused on the same plane i.e. tabletop, during the greater length of the track.

Background The setting against which the action takes place or any distant parts of a scene.

Background Plate (150) A processed picture print (usually of low contrast) used for back projection, front projection, bi-pack and aerial-image work.

Backlash Slop in the control gear of the compound. Its effect is minimised when the starting position on each control is arrived at by moving in the same direction as will be required for the shot.

Back-Light (88) (90) A light placed under the animation table. It enables the photography of transparencies, silhouettes of drawings or cels and bi-pack printing.

Back Projection (104) (112) Projects an image (via a front-silvered mirror) from below the animation table. Suitable material is placed below the cels on the table cut-out. (See also **Aerial Image**).

Barn Doors (84) Metal flaps hinged around the perimeter of a light source to control its beam.

Bar Sheet A chart showing detailed breakdown of the soundtrack in relation to each frame of the film.

Bi-Pack (102) The use of two strips of film in contact with each other (usually emulsion to emulsion) in a camera or projector gate.

Bi-Pack Magazine (102) A four-chamber magazine which enables two rolls of film to be fed to, and taken up from a camera or projector.

Bi-Pack Printing (102) A piece of processed film is fed through the camera gate in contact with raw, unexposed stock. Clear light rreaching the camera gate prints the image on the processed film onto the unexposed film.

Bleed The area of artwork extending beyond the area which will be photographed by the camera.

Bleeding Background action showing through a superimposition due either to an insufficently dense matte or inadequate exposure. Or unwanted material showing around the edges of static or travelling mattes and wipes due to misalignment or poor camera registration.

Burning In (98) Superimposing white outlines or lettering over a scene. The artwork (on a black background) is filmed on a separate pan through the camera. The black does not effect the other scene, the white 'burns' through it.

Cam (32) (See **Follow Focus Cam**).

Camera Aperture (28) An opening in the camera gate which masks off the unwanted area of the image produced by the lens before it reaches the film.

Capping Shutter (40) An additional shutter placed in front or behind the lens and operated independently of the normal camera shutter. Used during rewinds, ship-framing and cycling; essential when a cel-cycle is used during a fade or a mix.

Cels (10) Transparent plastic sheets used as a base onto which animation artwork is traced and painted.

Coaxial Lens (30) A lens mounted in such a way that its axis varies from the normal position of 90° to the focusing plane in the camera.

Colour Temperature (92) Measure of the colour of a light source by relating it to theoretically perfect (black body) source of radiant energy. The colour changes from reddish to bluish as the temperature, measured in kelvins (k) rises.

Colour Temperature Meter (97) A device for measuring the colour temperature.

Colour Separation Filters (100) Primary blue, red and green filters, used for obtaining a back-and-white record of the component colours of a colour scene.

Composite Image The assembly of different elements of a scene into one final picture.

Compound Move (64) A move requiring two or more simultaneous movements to be executed simultaneously.

Condensers (106) Two plano-convex condensers are used in aerial image projection. (See also **Aerial Image**).

Contrast Ratio The relationship between the darkest and the lightest areas of a scene. Depends on subject reflectance and lighting balance. Film type and processing can be varied to suit scene and result.

Counter-Matte (144) A matte which is the opposite shape to another matte; it is one of a matching pair.

Cutting Copy A workprint.

Density The relative opacity of developed photographic emulsion.

Depth of Field (34) Area of acceptably sharp focus in front of and beyond the plane of primary focus. It is determined by the focal length of the lens, *f*-stop, and the position of the primary focus. (See also **Hyperfocal Distance**).

Diaphragm (See **Iris**).

Diffusion (38) Reduction of image sharpness over part or the whole picture area by means of filters placed in front of the lens. Or softening the beam of light by the use of fibre-glass, spunglass, wire-mesh or similar material in front of the light source.

DIN Speed (94) Logarithmic film sensitivity measure, as defined in a German industrial standard.

Dissolve (42) (See **Mix**).

Double Exposure Two images photographed on the same piece of film. For a 50-50 ratio between two images of similar densities, each one is exposed one stop under the normal exposure.

Dope Sheet (118) Camera instruction sheet.

Drop Shadow A black shadow, corresponding to the outlines of lettering, obscuring part of the negative. When the lettering is added it can be tinted any colour. A larger shadow shifted slightly to one side of the lettering remains visible and can improve legibility on difficult backgrounds.

Emulsion Light-sensitive material supported on a permanent base such as film.

Emulsion Speed (94) The sensitivity of a photographic emulsion to light. It is usually measured in A.S.A. or DIN.

Exponential Zoom (70) The image size is increased (or decreased) at a constant rate throughout the full length of the track (zoom).

Exposure (94) (96) (108) Letting light reach a photographic emulsion. The effect of the exposure depends on the intensity of the light source; reflecting properties of the subject; lens *f* stop; camera exposure speed; as emulsion speed.

Exposure Meter (94) A device for measuring the intensity of light incidents on or reflecting from an object or scene. Meters normally have an exposure meter built in.

Exposure Speed (94) The length of time (usually in fractions of a second) that each frame of a film is exposed to light.

Fade (42) A progressive opening or closing of a variable shutter on the camera will cause the scene being photographed to appear from the black (fade in) or disappear into black (fade out).

Fairing (60) (62) (76) Speeding up and slowing out at the start and the end of a moving shot to soften the transition from and to static holds.

***f* Stop** (34) The relative lens aperture. All lenses transmit a similar proportion of light at the same *f* stop.

Field Chart (16) (66) A chart of the camera positions for particular field sizes with a given lens and format.

Field Size (16) (66) The area actually photographed.

Film Clip A short strip of motion picture film.

Filter Factor A number indicating the exposure compensation needed because of the absorbtion of light by a filter. The exposure time (without the filter) is multiplied by the factor for the particular filter.

Filter Mount (29) A support for glass or gelatine filters in front of the camera lens.

Fish-Eye Lens (36) Extreme wide angle lens which sacrifices rectilinear reproduction for its increased angular view, so introducing visible barrel distortion.

Flash Frame (144) A frame of film exposed to a white card; it represents a sync point.

Floating Peg Bar (56) An independent set of pegs suspended close to the surface of the table. Normally supplied with their own movement compound.

Flop-Over Box (132) (See **Matte Box**).

Focal Length (30) The distance between the centre of a lens and the point at which the image of a distant object comes into critical focus. In practical terms this also relates to the angle of view or angle of acceptance of a lens; i.e. a lens of longer focal length has a narrow angle of view than a lens of shorter focal length when used for a particular film format.

164

Focal Plane The plane at which the image is brought into critical focus; it is the plane occupied by the film.

Focus–Pull Altering the position of any primary focus of the lens, to maintain focus, or to make the scene go out of focus.

Focusing Plane The plane of the primary focus which lies perpendicular to the lens axis.

Follow Focus (32) Maintaining focus on the same plane (or subject) as the camera moves closer or farther from it. (See also **Auto-Focus**).

Follow Focus Cam (32) A cam cut to respond to the focusing curve of a specific lens. It is connected to the camera lens through a series of levels.

Foot Candle A unit for measuring the intensity of light. It represents the luminous intensity of one standard candle on a surface foot square placed at a distance of one foot from the candle.

Frame (24) Individual picture on a piece of motion picture film.

Framing (16) Selecting an area of the artwork to be photographed by the camera.

Freeze-Frame (10) Repeated printing of one frame of a motion picture film. The action appears to 'freeze' at that point.

Front Projection (114) Projecting a still or moving picture along the lens axis onto a highly reflective material in the subject plane. The image is reflected by a semi-silvered mirror in front of the camera lens.

Full Aperture (28) The full 35mm frame area, defined by suitable masking in the camera gate. (See also **Academy Aperture**).

Gate (28) Part of a camera or projector mechanism which holds the film during exposure or projection.

Gate Aperture (See **Aperture**).

Gel Coloured material (once gelatin) for colouring a light source (or for blacklit artwork).

Graticule (26) The frame outline engraved on the ground glass in the camera viewfinder. Can include any suitable framing or lining up information.

Grey Scale (96) A chart of grey strips which progressively cover the full range of tonal values from white to black.

Hard Edge Matte (130) A matte with a clearly defined edge, i.e. sharp focus.

Hi-Con A monochromatic emulsion on a clear base which has a very high contrast ratio between the black and white tones when processed. (Grey tones tend to disappear).

Hold (10) A cessation of camera or artwork movement for a number of frames.

In-Betweening (12) Preparing drawings to cover the action between the key animation positions.

Intermittent Movement The necessary film movement for taking or projecting motion pictures. Each frame is held steady for exposure or projection and moved between frames.

Iris A variable aperture controlling the amount of light passing through the lens; a scale on the outside of the lens is calibrated in *f* stops.

Jitter (124) (See **Strobing**).

Kelvin (92) The unit of temperature measurement used for colour temperature.

Key Light (86) The principle light used for the illumination of a subject.

Kilowatt (kW) (84) One thousand watts.

Logarithmic Zoom (70) Zoom rate calculated so that the subject size appears to change. A constant zoom rate does *not* have that effect – the zoom should.

Matte (144) Any opaque object which prevents the light reaching the film in a specific area of the frame; it can be placed at the artwork level, in front of the lens, behind the lens or in the camera (or projector) gate. (See **Travelling Matte**).

Mix (42) An optical transition; as the outgoing scene gradually disappears it is replaced by the incoming one.

Married Print A piece of motion picture film containing both the picture and the soundtrack.

Marry-Up (146) Joining together various elements of a composite shot.

Multiple Exposure The film is run through the gate of the camera several times and on each occasion a new element is photographed on the same piece of film.

Music Breakdown (120) The precise position of the relative beats, phrases or individual instruments in relationship to each frame of film.

Optical Effect A shot produced other than by straightforward conventional photography.

Opticals A general term encompassing mixes, fades, superimpositions, double-exposures, split-screens, freeze frames, skip frame and other optical effects.

Optical Sound Track A narrow band which carries the sound record optically printed.

Panchromatic Emulsion A black and white film emulsion which is sensitive to all colours.

Pantograph Table (54) A small, flat table attached to the size of the animation stand. A pointer attached to the shooting table indicates its position or suitable registered field charts or shot keys.

Peg Bar (48) A metal strip with three pins used for registering animation artwork; normally the middle pin is round and the other two flat. It may be fixed or travelling, when it is moved by a to pan the artwork attached to it. A series of found and flat pegs can be screwed into specific positions along the peg bar to which the artwork is registered. (See also Floating Peg Bar).

Pic-Sync A machine used for synchronising one or more sound-tracks to the motion picture film during the editing process.

Platen (18) A piece of glass, loose or hinged to the stand, to press down flat any artwork to be photographed.

Projector Aperture (104) An opening in the projector gate which masks off all unwanted light from the projector bulb so that only a specific frame area is projected by the lens.

Puncher (48) A machine used for punching registration holes in animation cels and other artwork.

Push–Off Wipe (130) A wipe that gives the effect that one scene is pushed out of the screen area by another which replaces it.

Rack-Over Viewfinder (24) A camera viewfinder which allows a scene to be viewed through the taking lens only for lining up when the camera body is moved over to one side.

Raw Stock Unexposed film.

Reflex Viewfinder (24) A camera viewfinder which allows a scene to be viewed through the taking lens.

Registration Pegs (48) (See **Peg Bars**).

Registration Pins (110) (**Pilot Pins**) Static or moving pins which form part of a camera or projector gate and which are used to engage the film perforations and hold each frame in register during exposure or projection.

Reversal Stock Motion picture emulsion which gives a positive image of the scene photographed.

Rotoscope (26) (136) Device used to project an image from a camera. It can show a graticule or film clip in the camera viewfinder or in the camera gate.

Shot Key (116) A sheet of semi-transparent paper which is registered to the artwork it relates to, and which carries the frame outlines of the start and end positions of a camera move.

Shot Planning (46) (122) (140) A plotting out of camera moves.

Single Frame Exposures (40) The exposure of one frame of motion picture film at a time.

Soft Edge Matte An out of focus matte.

Sound Breakdown The precise position of the relevant sounds such as music, voices, sound effects etc. in relationship to each other as well as to each frame of film.

Speech Breakdown The precise position of each individual syllable in relation to each frame of the film.

Storyboard A series of sketches indicating the proposed treatment of a shot or a series of shots.

Synchronisation (118) The matching up of sound and picture.

Sync Mark A specific frame which acts as a zero point for the start of a shot; it also represents the synchronisation point between a piece of film and a soundtrack or other piece of film with which it may eventually be combined.

Travelling Mattes (138) Mattes prepared on high contrast motion picture stock and used in the camera in contact with the raw stock. They change from frame to frame as dictated by the scene being shot.

Whip Pan (64) (124) A very fast pan from one position to another. The in-between frames appear blurred.

Wipe (128) (130) An optical effect whereby one scene is progressively replaced by another with the appearance of a wipe line where the two images meet.

Zoom (124) The zooming effect is achieved on an animation stand by tracking the camera towards or away from the subject being photographed.

Zoom Lens A lens with focal length continuously variable within a specific range. It can change the image size without the camera moving.